Foreword

'What I needed to know when I first went to school' is a vital book for both students and parents as they start to embark on the transition to secondary school.

I have worked alongside Phil Priestley for many years, initially when he was a community police sergeant, supporting local schools, and more recently through his organization, 'Inclusive Development', which provides crucial support to vulnerable students.

Phil's dedication to the welfare of young people is truly inspiring. Over the years, I have witnessed the positive impact he has made on countless young lives, helping them to understand and overcome the challenges they face to achieve their potential. His previous experience as a police officer has given him a unique insight into the issues that many young people face, enriching his work in schools, where he has developed effective and inventive strategies to help them tackle their problems.

Phil also founded the Cambs Youth Panel, providing a platform for young people to have their voices heard, where they can influence council policy decisions that affect the lives of young people. Participating in such panels also gives them invaluable experience of working within a team, enhancing their communication skills by coherently debating with each other, as well as in public speaking.

Starting secondary school is a major milestone in the educational life of young students. It can be an exhilarating time, but it can also be stressful and daunting. Compared to their primary schools, for many the sheer scale of secondary schools can be intimidating. Add to that the unfamiliar routines, the diverse social groups, and the new academic expectations they face, its small wonder some can find the transition overwhelming.

Philip Priestley's book provides an invaluable resource to help young people navigate the challenges of embarking into secondary school. He encourages them to reflect on their relationships with those around them, particularly with their teachers, and regard them not as figures of authority but as allies in their educational journey, to see them as human beings with the same strengths and weakness we all have. Further chapters cover a range of issues to help the young readers navigate their secondary school experience, including making friends, conflict resolution, stress management, addiction, and other adolescent challenges they might encounter. By providing practical solutions to such problems, Phil dispels any trepidation they might feel by empowering them with the confidence to manage their adolescent years.

One of the striking features of the book lies in its presentation. Phil uses two fictional characters, Katie and Jez, to guide his readers through the various topics he explores. This accessible approach makes the book relatable for young people, because the characters reflect their own feelings and experiences. His deft use of humour and astute observations help ease any anxieties his young readers may have, while subtly encouraging them to seek help if they need it. Each chapter concludes with a check-list of its key points that succinctly summarises what he wants his readers to think about.

Every day as a teacher, I see my students struggling to cope with the pressures of school and the complex demands of modern life. Phil's book provides a much-needed resource of support and guidance for young people about to head into secondary school, and for any parents anxious about how their child will cope with the transition. By providing practical advice on a range of topics and scenarios in such a relatable way, he equips his readers with the tools to successfully navigate the next stage of their educational journey, and in doing so, to fulfil their potential.

Lastly, on a personal note, thank you, Phil, for your tireless work in support of young people and for sharing your perception and wisdom in this book.

Forward by Dominic Fullman

Deputy Principal, Bottisham Village College (Anglian Learning Trust).

Introduction

Hi – I'm Phil. I'm the author of this book and I've written a couple of other books (which were about criminal gangs). I was a police officer for 17 years and I left the police to work full time in schools supporting children and young people across the upper part of primary school (key stage 2) and all the way through their GCSEs.

The work that I do is about helping young people to make the most of their gifts and their talents. I've spent a lot of time working one to one mentoring and coaching young people. They bring me their challenges and we talk them through and find a way to solve those problems.

This book reflects the issues and the problems that I help young people to confront on a day-to-day basis. These are the problems that you might encounter yourself – particularly as you move up from Primary School to Secondary school and on into your exams.

You probably won't encounter *all* of the problems in this book – everyone is different – but some of the problems lead into each other and overlap with other things. The good news is that, very often, if you find a solution to one problem, another problem will also go away. More good news: The solutions are usually easier and less difficult than you think they are going to be! This book is about two things. Firstly, I'll be offering you some of the solutions that have worked for other people in similar situations. Secondly, it's also about helping you to improve your problem-solving skills too so that you can be more independent.

Don't ever worry about asking for help, looking for help, or trying things that work for other people. There is nothing written down that says you have to solve all your own problems on your own. You don't have to come up with new solutions that nobody has ever seen before! Trust me – life is not like that. Surround yourself with good, honest and positive people that you can believe in, and look for good examples. Never be afraid to talk, never feel ashamed to fail, we all get things wrong. You have to fail sometimes to know how to succeed. Sometimes you don't really value your success until you've been through the painful experience of not getting what you want.

Above all else, I want you to believe in yourself!

I basically do not believe that anyone wants to fail or experience failure. I believe that everyone wants to succeed. You want to enjoy a positive life with uplifting experiences. Success looks like different things for different people, but whatever success means to you, *I want you to know that you can get it.*

No matter what your background is you will have challenges to overcome (everybody does). It's very easy to look over at someone else and feel that they have it easier than you do. You might think that they are more gifted, or that their family has more money, that they are funnier or better looking, or better at sports, or better in classes... believe me some people look at you and feel the same sense of envy for your gifts and advantages. It is also true to say that some people *have* got bigger challenges to confront and overcome, but everything is relative. That is to say, what one person finds to be easy, another person finds very difficult or nearly impossible.

In this book I love a practical example, so let's have a look at one! If you asked me to dunk a basketball I genuinely couldn't go and do that *right now*!

My guess is that if I trained hard in the gym and I took coaching and followed the advice – *and if I really wanted to enough* – I probably could learn to dunk a basketball. I have no idea how long it would take, but I could get there. It's always easier for me to list the reasons why I probably *wouldn't* achieve that though.

Muggsy Bogues was a professional NBA basketball player between 1987 and 2001, but unlike all the other players Muggsy was kind of short. I don't mean short for the NBA – like 6'2" or something – Muggsy was 5'3" tall. The average height of an NBA player is 6'6" tall, but there were players like Shaquille O'Neal playing against Muggsy, and he was 7'1". That's nearly two feet taller! Not only did Muggsy play *14 professional seasons* of basketball in the best league in the world – he dunked!

Somethings make you more likely to succeed, and somethings make you less likely to succeed. Having self-awareness[1] is the first step towards achieving your goals. You must be honest with yourself about what your weaknesses are so that you can work hard to improve on

---

[1] Knowledge of yourself and about you.

them. Then you have to be aware of what you're good at, and what your strengths are. Where possible you'll use those strengths to your own advantage so that people see the best version of you.

Sometimes people tell you that you have to 'let go of your excuses'. *I need to tell you that I don't hold with that.* Some of the things that might make your success *less likely* are things that define you and make you who you are. You might even draw a certain amount of strength from your adversity. It's not about denying those things, suppressing those things or 'letting them go'. You need to know what they are and how they disadvantage you, but you need to recognise them, and you need to work with them to find your success.

There are things in life that we call 'protective factors' and there are things that we call 'risk factors'. Broadly speaking these things have been the subject of lots of academic research. A 'protective factor' is something that makes things better and improves your chances of success. A 'risk factor' is something that makes your success less likely (or might pose a risk to you). What is confusing is that sometimes a 'risk factor' can also *help you* – it might make you stronger and it can improve your resilience (resilience is that thing that keeps you going no matter how hard it gets). With nothing to test you, and everything in your favour – sometimes the smallest challenge can trip you up when it finally does arrive, because you simply don't recognise it or know how to cope with it.

I don't like the word 'excuses' either. An excuse is very close to a lie in my opinion, a lie we tell ourselves or others to get ourselves some sympathy for not doing well. Being honest with yourself about why things didn't work is not about 'excuses'. You need to love yourself whether you are winning or losing, and never lose that personal belief that you can take yourself forward.

I want this book to be easy to read, relatable and realistic. I want it to be enjoyable. I want to use lots of examples, practical examples from the schools that I work in, but also other examples that might involve highly successful people that you may or may not have heard about.

It is very easy to look at someone when they are at the peak of their success and think that they were just 'born that way'. Take an Olympic gold medal winner. That person might be stood on the top of that podium listening to the national anthem of their country, they look incredible, they are a champion, but if you go back through their history, there was a time when they weren't. There was a time when they were late for school. There was a time when they thought their dream wasn't going to happen. They had moments of self-doubt and pain to deal with. Nobody ever came along and told them what the future had in store for them – or promised them the outcome of an Olympic gold medal. *They built themselves in the image of a champion.* They went after their dream. At one time though – they just walked down the street like everyone else, and nobody knew their name.

I want you to think about your name – and we're going to consider that. That name is your brand. It becomes so closely associated with what you do that before anything else, your name creates anticipation, it makes people expect a certain something. You know how brands work – we all do. We can all name the strong brands like Apple, Nike, Louis Vuitton, Gucci, all these brands work incredibly hard to impress a certain customer, to convince people that they are worth buying (or working hard to buy). You have to start thinking about who *you* are trying to impress – and what is it that you want to convince people of?

This book is something that might be read by someone who is coming up from primary school and who is looking to make a great start in their new secondary school. You might be further into your educational journey and already established in secondary school. You might be a high achiever who wants to build on the success that you've already begun to enjoy. You might be someone who has been through a lot of difficulty – either in primary school or in the first couple of years at secondary school – and you want to change that. You might be someone who is tired of not doing as well as you think that you ought to be doing. Whatever your situation – the very fact that you're picking up a book like this shows that you're ready to start thinking about investing in yourself in a different way.

Don't expect this book to give you some kind of smooth, easy, fast track that just wins and never loses. In any route to success, you will experience ups and downs, there will be setbacks and there will be massively encouraging experiences that carry you forward too. This book might help you to develop a more effective route to your goals, and I hope that it will help you to appreciate your successes and your setbacks in a more balanced way – but ultimately your success will be all yours.

With my best wishes to you and thanks for reading my book,

Phil

Chapter 1:
Teachers are People!

What a strange place to begin! 'All teachers are people!'.

You might think "Well duh... yeah of course!". You say that, but how many people are surprised when they see one of their teachers somewhere ordinary – like in the supermarket?

You know the situation. You're in the supermarket, maybe with your Mum, possibly with your friends, just keeping your head down on the cereal aisle minding your own business.

All of a sudden, there's Miss Peterson, your geography teacher and she's buying... 'Cheerios'... and now you know what Miss Peterson has for breakfast! OMG. She has a basket and there's all sorts of stuff in there...

BUT WHAT'S THIS NOW?

Mr Richards, the *actual* French teacher Mr Richards, who sometimes stands in for P.E. has wandered round from the other aisle and he has put something in Miss Peterson's basket. *What is actually going on here??*

He just literally *tossed* a jar of Douwe Egberts instant coffee into Miss Peterson's basket! That's the expensive coffee too! Perhaps there is a beef between Miss Peterson and Mr Richards and Mr Richards is trying to hyperinflate the price of Miss Peterson's groceries by putting the super expensive brands into her basket without her knowing. *What a snake!*

BUT THEN – *O M G* – HE IS HOLDING HER ACTUAL HAND NOW! BREAKING NEWS! YOU HAVE JUST SEEN MISS

PETERSON AND MR RICHARDS HOLDING HANDS IN TESCOS!!

It was enough to realise that Miss Peterson eats breakfast cereal and shops in a supermarket – but this is a whirlwind of information right now. Your brain is practically snapping, crackling and popping alongside these Rice Krispies here…

Oh my days.

So you briefly contemplate taking a photo on your phone – but you don't because that would be so wrong and creepy, and then you wonder how anyone would possibly even believe you and then you realise your friends are just in the next aisle – or maybe you can get your Mum - because if your Mum sees it too she can back you to your friends when they come round your house…

So you run down the cereal aisle, swing a hard skidding left and bump into your mate Jezza and you breathlessly say

"Miss Peterson… cheerios… Ricardo… [Mr Richards nickname behind his back] Douwe Egberts coffee… trolley… HOLDING HANDS!!!"

"AT FIRST I THOUGHT THEY HAD GROCERIES RELATED BEEF BUT THEN HE *HELD HER HAND*!"

"YOU HAVE TO SEE THIS! YOU HAVE TO SEE THIS!"

So you and Jezza run back round into the cereal aisle and… **they're gone**.

Jezza is like "OK you got me"

"No it's real Jez I swear down – on my Mum's life"

"Nah – it never happened – great story though"

"No come on they have to still be here – we can find them"

So the search of Sainsbury's begins [other supermarkets are available]. You and Jez search Sainsbury's together, but you can't split up because you know that means you'll find them and then you won't be able to find Jezza and then you'll find Jezza but you won't find them again… it's too much stress right now!!

Maybe you should have taken that photo? NO DEFINITELY NOT THAT WAS SUCH A WRONG IDEA.

Having run out of energy you and Jez sit on the floor as Miss Peterson and Mr Richards (Ricardo) float noiseless past, behind your backs, and you don't even see them as they pack their weekly shopping into the boot of his car.

When you get back to school on Monday you cannot wait – cannot wait – to see what is going on.

You walk down the corridor and here's Miss Peterson walking ahead of you… and there's Ricardo walking towards you… OH IT'S HAPPENING NOW!

And then Ricardo says "Hi" casually to Miss Peterson and she nods and they just keep walking. It's as if the whole situation in Sainsbury's never even happened. *Did it even happen?*

Do you think that Sainsbury's would actually give you the CCTV? On the requirement of your mental health? Your whole credibility might depend on this. *Not even Jezza believes you.*

This whole story might sound pretty far-fetched. I guess for comedy purposes – it is, slightly. It's not *that* far-fetched though.

Working in a school I do sometimes bump into kids who know me, or at least recognise me, from one of the schools I'm working in. They might get really shy – way more shy than they ever would be in school – or they might pluck up the courage to come up and say "Hi Sir" (nobody ever calls me 'Sir' outside school).

"So you do shopping?"

"Yes Gaz, I also do shopping. Do you do shopping?"

"Yes Sir. I'm also doing shopping"

[Awkward]

The thing is – it is really hard to think of this person that you see in school out of their context. That is to say, outside of the boundaries of their school.

"Sir you're wearing a hoodie"

"Yes I am, do you like it?"

Teachers often get seen as some type of educational robot. They are confined to their specific classroom, maybe a couple of adjoining corridors, a staffroom and the areas they do lunch duty in.

You know that your P.E. teacher has knees because you've seen them when he or she wears shorts in the summer. *But Mr Wallis?* The grumpy strict teacher who says things like "The bell is for me, not for you" and "It's your own time you're wasting" and who practically enjoys giving out after school detentions? *Nah – that bloke sleeps under his desk.* Or they switch him off at night and put him on charge in the cupboard...

When you say "Teachers are people" – you might respond "Well duh, of course". So why are you surprised to see them doing human things and being humans? You have to realise at the very outset that all of your teachers are human – all of them! That makes them very different individually. They have private hopes and fears. They have challenges in their lives. They have aspirations – that is – believe it or not, things that they want to achieve and experience too. Their life isn't over – just like you, they are living their life. They might be planning their own skiing holiday for the winter, and they are just living for the week they are going to get on the snow in France. They might be working on a car at home that they are rebuilding from the chassis up – but one day, it's going to be a restored 1972 Porsche 911 in factory original tangerine paint. It's really expensive though so it is taking ages and at the moment it looks like nothing. Maybe they care for sick animals and a significant amount of their wages goes into supporting stables for injured horses? They might one day hope that their efforts will find a way to allow them to go full time – as much as they do love teaching – they'd love to work with the animals all day.

Different teachers have different views and opinions across a range of subjects. Some teachers like each other, and some teachers don't. Some teachers are best friends. Some teachers get together and end up married.

Teachers are parents too. Some have kids – sometimes in your school one of the kids has a parent who is a teacher. Sometimes the teachers have kids in other schools. Just like all parents they think about their kids all day – they worry about them and hope that is everything is going ok. They have to find the money to buy the Nike Air Force 1s that have just gone up in price for everyone, or the cost of the school trip.

The question is – do we treat our teachers as people?

The Times Educational Supplement [2] – one the largest industry magazines for schools and teachers – published a report in 2021 saying that 10% of teachers (so that's one teacher in every ten) has been threatened with violence by a student.

This report also says that students have found teachers online and taunted them with abuse and harassment.

---

[2] https://www.tes.com/magazine/news/general/1-10-teachers-threatened-violence-pupils

In this report 6% of teachers said that they had actually been attacked by a student – and a huge 40% - which is very nearly half of all teachers – said that they had been verbally abused.

This is very sad indeed.

The truth is – if it were any other section of society abusing any other group of people to such an extent, it wouldn't be acceptable at all. That is to say – *it is unacceptable* – but, for some reason, we have come to accept it.

Some students reading this book will turn on me as an author now, particularly if they realise that they have been unkind to a teacher, and they'll say "Yeah but _____ [insert that teacher's name] was *asking for it*" or "They started it" or "Shouldn't have talked to me like they did".

In any other context – if we were talking about domestic abuse (like a boyfriend mistreating his girlfriend for example) we would definitely call that 'victim blaming'.

Now behind those statistics we know that *not all students* (are we seeing a parallel here to other types of abuse?) are guilty of this wrongdoing. Of course not, but in a class of thirty students it only takes one, or maybe two students and that teacher does receive that abuse. 28 innocent students in that session (and maybe over six classes in one day, 175 blameless students), but for that teacher they received abuse that day. And the next day. *And the next day*. Not always from the same person, not always for the same reason, but nonetheless day in and day out the teacher is being abused in his or her workspace.

One thing is for sure – it's a lot easier to abuse a teacher, if you don't see your teacher as a person.

Let's wind that clock back to Sainsbury's and to Miss Peterson and Mr Richards.

Miss Peterson and Mr Richards have been dating for eight months. They're really happy with each other. They're both young teachers – they're in their mid-twenties – and they moved in together last weekend. Today Miss Peterson got verbally abused by someone who didn't do his geography homework. He was sanctioned according to a scale that exists in the school code of conduct and he received an after-school detention. It's the third time this has happened, and Miss Peterson has tried different ways to get the

Miss Peterson is actually so nice! She's lovely!

student to do homework and hand it in on time. Miss Peterson gets held to account by her head of department and by the school principal if her students don't do their homework. *What is she doing about it?*

So Miss Peterson issued a detention – and yes – she raised her voice and was very direct about it.

Miss Peterson has worked hard to put her lessons together and this student has been disruptive and has undermined the hard work she has been doing – and the learning of other students.

So the student swore at Miss Peterson in a really nasty way. He also said something that was vaguely threatening and he made other people laugh at her, even if it was that uncomfortable nervous laughter, but the situation was really horrible.

At break time Miss Peterson was genuinely upset by what had happened. She had a cup of tea and she tried to put it behind her.

She sent a message to Mr Richards saying *"I didn't think teaching would be like this – this isn't why I became a teacher"*.

That evening Mr Richards tried to make Miss Peterson feel better. He held her hand. He told her that she was a good teacher…

Now if you understand that teachers are people – you also understand that they have emotions, and that they have good days and bad days. You know that different things motivate them. You know that different things impress them.

You also need to understand that you won't click with every teacher that teaches you and you shouldn't try to go out of your way to be the student that every teacher likes. This isn't about that.

By the way - *do you not think that teachers see the kids who are being fake?*

Just like you – if a teacher meets someone who is not sincere and comes across as fake – they're going to be wary of that.

"Oh hi Miss your hair is just *so lovely*" (Miss knows that she is tired and this morning she barely brushed her hair).

It's all a bit much. Nobody is recommending that.

The truth is that successful students treat teachers as people – and that means seeing things from their perspective and being thoughtful towards them.

I meet a lot of people who think that they are feuding with a teacher.

"Oh yeah – me and Mr Williams – we got beef".

You think so?

"Mr Williams definitely hates me – always has – I don't know why, but we got beef."

Now Mr Williams could be a very experienced teacher – maybe 40 years old – been teaching 17 years. *What type of 40-year-old man has beef with a 13 year old boy?*

"I will never hand his homework in because I will not give him the satisfaction."

So Mr Williams continues to give this student after school detentions and sanctions and generally shows disapproval for the fact that the homework isn't being done.

In lessons the student is cheeky and offensive. Talks behind his hand. Tries to make other people laugh. Has no intention of learning from what is being presented.

In his mind, the student has created what we call 'a narrative'. It's a story that supports his misbehaviour. The student and the teacher are at 'crossed purposes'[3]. The teacher is trying to get everyone – not just this student – to pass an exam. To do that he needs them to 'buy in' and try to get the work done. The harder they try the better they get. As the old saying goes "I've always been lucky – but the harder I try, the luckier I get".

Meanwhile one student is working against the flow of that. This student has convinced himself that's it's actually about *him* – and that personal 'beef' that 'they' have.

Now, do not get me wrong – students can have a personal rapport with their teacher – and that rapport can be positive or negative. It grows and it develops over time. Sometimes

---

[3] Crossed purposes – they're trying to achieve different things.

that relationship can breakdown – but I guarantee you right now that no teacher is going to jeopardise their pension and their career to have a personal beef with a student. Are they going to seek you out on social media?

"Yo fam – you not doing your trigonometry? How you gonna dis my home boy Pythagoras like that? You just gonna do him dirty? You don't even know how to find to the length of the hypotenuse – your game is so weak."

Instead the teacher brings the class in and wearily faces another hour of just one student in the class making life hard for everyone with some bad jokes and a flavour of personal disrespect.

Seeing your teacher as a person is about having the courage and the honesty to get on the level with them.

"Sir can I see you after the class – would that be ok?"

The teacher might say "I'm really sorry I've got to be somewhere at the end of the lesson" (they might have to get across the school to sub for another teacher – you just don't know – trust me, they won't be super happy about that either) but the strong likelihood is that either they will say "Sure – that would be great" or they'll otherwise say "Why don't you come back and see me at..." and give you a bit of their time.

So you get to see your teacher, and on the level, you say:

"Look – numbers have always troubled me and I struggle with it. Also things at home are complicated and it's hard to

get the head space to do homework. I know I miss a lot of stuff. I just wanted you to know that I'll try – but it's definitely not easy – and if I miss things, I'm not disrespecting you. I do appreciate your time."

I'm telling you now – if your circumstances resemble what I just described there – your teacher would not only be surprised to hear you speak in that way, they will be impressed in a massive way.

There is nothing about that which suggests that you are being insincere. You're treating your teacher as a human being and a person. You don't expect them to know your story or your situation – so you're explaining.

Most teachers will respond in such a positive way to the courage that it takes to be open and honest like that. I would expect them to say "Is there anything I can do to help you with that situation?" or at the very least "Is there anything you'd like to tell me about?".

Fundamentally all good teachers want you to be safe – before anything else. Safe and well.

"You know Sir, I don't always eat breakfast and I have to look after my Dad because he's disabled – that's not easy."

"Do you know about the young carers team that we have in the school?"

"No I don't think I'd like that."

"Well maybe we could find out – I could get you some information – you don't have to go along there but they *understand what you're going through and they can give you lots of things to help you out."*

Is this the teacher that you've been having 'beef' with for the last two years?

What you didn't realise was that, well, you want to be a car mechanic and get an apprenticeship and actually, Sir has been rebuilding that Porsche 911 since you were three years old...

Now I'm not saying this because I'm super biased (ok I am super biased I guess) – but teachers are usually wonderful people. Genuinely. Most teachers have qualifications and a range of personal experiences that mean that they could apply for other jobs and roles that pay more than teachers get paid. Teachers do not get paid what they should and it's a global issue[4]. You can go to most developed (and for that matter undeveloped) nations and there will either be a teacher shortage or the teachers are underpaid.

There are examples of teachers in the public school system of the United States who have given blood in return for payment to make their bills add up at the end of the month. They have sold their blood. To carry on teaching.

It is not rewarded with huge financial sums, there have been pay freezes and pension reforms since 2008, teachers have been receiving increasing amounts of verbal and physical abuse, and yet – still – despite all this, people with degrees

---

[4] True all over the world.

in maths, sciences, international languages, still want to educate and support young people.

Some of the most incredible people I have met in my working life have been teachers. Are they wearing the most fashionable clothes? Driving the fanciest cars? Living in the big houses? No. Almost certainly not. In fact, I would suggest that one or two of them have no excuse for how bad their dress sense actually is (but that's another point – seriously – in one or two cases it must be deliberate) but in terms of the most sincere and heartfelt of people, the least selfish? If I had to pick out a group of people to get stuck with on a desert island – all I'm saying is that I wouldn't be choosing the investment bankers from the London stock exchange. I'm going to get on that island with a group of teachers – they're resourceful, they have a great sense of humour (don't believe me? You have to trust me on this), and they work hard. These guys are very special. None of us would be where we are without the teachers that helped us to become who we are. The doctors, the nurses, the lawyers, yes – the investment bankers and the business-people – all of us.

So where does it all begin? This treating teachers like human beings thing?

Well – start prompting yourself to think about them as you would the other people in your life. Not as educational robots, but as people. You see that your teacher has a cold – quietly ask them if they're ok? Offer them a tissue if you have one?

When you see them in the corridor, or you go into their classroom, maybe say good morning, and try to be cheerful. Show them respect, and demonstrate that you respect them by just being polite.

Have you ever said "Thank you Miss" on your way out of the classroom? I really do hope so, because you have no idea how much that actually means to a teacher.

Have you ever told a teacher that you enjoyed that lesson or that the lesson was good?

When you do something that you enjoy in a lesson, have you ever thought to say to your teacher "I like it when we get to do a practical demonstration" (or whatever it was) "I like it when we get to do creative writing"?

Your teachers are definitely not against you. Think of it this way – if they are successful it is because their class does well. If they get a great set of GCSE results they get congratulated and they are viewed as a really outstanding teacher. Now it's not all about the results – but sometimes a great teacher will take a student who has low personal expectations and is surrounded by a perception[5] that, for one reason or another, they are not going to do well. Working with that student they secure a pass mark – a solid pass mark. That student and that teacher worked hard together, they believed in each other, and they set a goal. They worked against expectations, they took it one step at a

---
[5] Idea or understanding that they have formed.

time, and in that subject, that student went into that GCSE exam and they got a grade 5.

The absolute truth is that, despite whatever you might think, most teachers love to help a student achieve a grade 9 (of course they do), but seeing a young person with low expectations push themselves to get a GCSE grade 5 and pass the subject? *That's actually where the reward is.* You take a high flying, super motivated, and highly gifted student and they get a 9 – how much of that is genuinely credited to the teacher? There is a suspicion that you could give that student to most teachers and you would hope that they would get a similar outcome. When you take a student who is unsure of themselves, who is struggling in lots of subjects, maybe there have been behavioural problems in the past, and that student has had low academic achievement their whole time at school. You take *that* student, and you work with them, and you ride out the ups and the downs, and you believe in them when they don't believe in themselves, and maybe even when they self-sabotage and do silly things... but you *stick with it*, you refuse to give up and you work and work and have their back the whole time. Then that student lands a 5 in the exam. They were predicted a 3 or a 4 – but they went in and they slam-dunked a 5. Honestly – teachers *live* for that. *You will never forget that teacher and that teacher will never forget you.*

So when we talk about being successful in school, no matter what your goals are, no matter what you want to achieve, let's begin *here*. With the teachers. The teachers are humans

– humans are flawed wonderful things. Some good, some not so good, you like some more than others. Treat all of your teachers with respect and dignity, be polite no matter how much you like them, be honest in a respectful way (you know exactly what I mean). It's easy to be polite and show dignity to people that you *like* – your real test is to do this with your teachers no matter how much you do or do not like them. Always respect teachers for who they are and what they do, for what they stand for and how much their contribution actually counts in our world and in our society.

The strongest and bravest, most mature thing you can ever do for a teacher is when someone in a class shows them disrespect or abuse - you either challenge that in a quietly dignified way like *"I don't think it's ok to speak to Miss like that – I might not always like her or agree with her, but I don't think that's ok"* (that is hugely brave) or just to go to the teacher at the end of the lesson and say *"I just want you to know that I didn't think that what happened there was ok"*.

Let's care for our teachers – let's care about our teachers – and let's understand that they are on our side and they are key to our success. *No teachers, no school.*

*By the way if you do see two of your teachers dating, don't gossip about them or take it to the internet. That's not cool.

Jez! I just found out that Miss Peterson and Mr Richards are... are...

PEOPLE!!!

(GULP!)

Teachers are people!:
Checklist:

- Are you polite to your teachers?
- Are you honest with your teacher?
- Do you ever think of your teacher as a part of someone's family?
- Do you ever check that your teacher is ok?
- Do you ever challenge unkind behaviour that is aimed at your teacher?
- Do you ever try to offer reassurance to your teacher if someone does or says something unpleasant to them in class?
- Do you respect their deadlines on things like homework?
- If they have to sanction you – do you accept it in a mature and respectful way?

Chapter 2:
Learning how to empathise

There are lots of things that we learn as we grow up. I want to focus on three things particularly.

I want you to understand that when you arrive at secondary school your brain is a long way from being fully developed. In fact – your brain won't stop developing to its full capability until you reach the age of about 25.

Along the way different parts of your brain develop and get stronger – giving you greater control of your range of emotions, provoking you to become more thoughtful and

Your brain won't stop developing until 9 years after you leave school!!!

probably less reactive to what is going on around you.

It is not uncommon for teenagers to be characterised[6] as impulsive, likely to experience mood swings, prone to anger management problems and possibly quite emotional. *Of course, not all teenagers are like this* and where it happens it usually happens for understandable reasons.

---

[6] Known to be or described as.

You might have heard your Mum or someone else say "It's hormones and puberty". Ok – ok, hormones are going to have a big impact on your mood too, and yes, as you move from 11 through to 16, your hormone levels are going to change *a lot* as well.

All of these things are part of a big and complicated picture that changes who you are – from the version of you that was a child, through the journey of your life into adulthood.

In addition to everything that is happening inside you on an emotional, psychological (mind), and physical level – there are hundreds of outside influences that change your views and your attitudes. *Who are your role models? Who do you listen to? What kind of diet do you eat? What is your neighbourhood like? What is your home life like?*

Even this book – as you read it now – is trying to influence you in some way, and it might do.

One of the biggest developments that young people go through as they mature into adulthood is learning that the world isn't all about them.

Sometimes it feels like you're the lead actor in a script – in a film – the film is your life and you're the central figure in that film. You might not have worked out what the film is or what's going to happen in it, but you feel that you're the most important figure in that film. Other people around you have important supporting roles – but you feel like the star. *Some of the other people that you encounter are frankly not very important because they don't play a big part in the whole script.*

I think some people would look at that and say — "That's quite an arrogant view of the world".

As we get older, hopefully we do learn to value ourselves — but we also learn to appreciate the importance of the people around us. It's not that other people are more important than we are — it's just that we realise that it's genuinely not all about us.

You are starting to form your sense of identity when you move to secondary school — *who is it that you want to be?* You might become more self-conscious about how other people view you during this period and some people become very shy, or possibly very loud and attention seeking... it's a difficult time. You want to feel secure and happy, you want to feel like you belong — but it's really not unusual to feel awkward, to feel uncertain, and to not really know what is going on.

A man named Erik Erikson — an incredibly clever German-American psychologist (that is, an expert on the way humans think) developed a model that has eight stages. It is called the 'eight stages of psychosocial development'.

[Ok stay with me here — we've got this!]

The eight stages map the different point of your life and maturity through the years that you live. Stage one begins in infancy (birth to 18 months old) and stage 8 happens from 65 years old onwards.

The stages that really matter to you right now are stages 4 and stages 5.

Stage 4 is what happens at the final years of primary school – the major questions that you ask yourself at this stage are "How can I be good at something?" and "Am I doing as well as everyone else?". The most important event is generally going to school and being successful there. During this time you are testing yourself and you start to feel good about the things that you are doing well. As you get to the top of Primary School you start to think "Hey I've got this!".

Stage 5 is where you move from primary school and into your teenage years. You start to ask yourself "Who am I?" and "What do I stand for?". Social relationships, finding your people, and having friendships that you can trust begin to take on a new level of importance at this stage. It is a confusing time. A minute ago, you were feeling really good about yourself – now you might start to doubt yourself a bit more and you might feel confused about what really matters in your life. *It is getting more complicated to simply be 'you'.*

Moving into these years you're going to be less self-focused and you're going to start recognising a whole world that surrounds you.

What I want you to start thinking about is the world from the other person's perspective – not just your own. Learning to do this is a major advantage and helps you to become so much more successful.

Seeing things from the view of other people happens in gradual ways.

A famous old phrase is:

"Before you judge a person, walk a mile in their shoes"

This saying is so old, and so often used, that people have really forgotten who exactly came up with this. Sometimes it is attributed to the wisdom of Native American tribes. I've also seen it attributed to a poem by Mary T Lathrap, written in 1895 – called "Judge Softly" (the poem is on the next couple of pages for you to read).

This message is all about one of the most powerful things that defines the best in humanity. Something that we also witness in other highly intelligent animals. *This is the ability to empathise.*

Empathy is something that is characterised in the wisdom of the elephant. The largest of land mammals - capable of huge destruction when angry, but also a very peaceful and loving creature that co-exists with so many other species of animals around it.

The truth is – it takes great power, and a huge amount of strength, to *empathise*. It is so much easier to be judgemental, to be petty or to be vengeful (that is the instinct to want to 'get your own back' on someone). Part of empathy is certainly forgiveness. Empathy is definitely an emotion that leads to forgiveness and to reconciliation (that is the healing of disagreements between people).

So what is this magic thing – this 'empathy'? What actually is it?

"Judge Softly"

"Pray, don't find fault with the man that limps,

Or stumbles up the road.

Unless you have worn the moccasins he wears,

Or stumbled beneath the same load.

"There may be tears in his soles that hurt

Though hidden from view.

The burden he bears placed on your back

May cause you to stumble and fall, too.

Don't sneer at the man who is down today

Unless you have felt the same blow

That caused his fall or felt the shame

That only the fallen know.

You may be strong, still the blows

That were his, unknown to you in the same way,

May cause you to stagger and fall, too.

Don't be too harsh with the man that sins.

Or pelt him with words, or stone, or disdain.

Unless you are sure you have no sins of your own,

And it's only wisdom and love that your heart contains.

For you know if the tempter's voice

Should whisper as soft to you,

As it did to him when he went astray,

It might cause you to falter, too.

Just walk a mile in his moccasins

Before you abuse, criticise and accuse.

If just for one hour, you could find a way

To see through his eyes instead of your own muse.

I believe you'd be surprised to see

That you've been blind and narrow-minded, even unkind.

There are people on reservations and in the ghettos

Who have so little hope, and too much worry on their minds.

Brother, there but for the grace of God go you and I.

Just for a moment, slip into his mind and traditions

And see the world through his spirit and eyes

Before you cast a stone or falsely judge his conditions.

Remember to walk a mile in his moccasins

And remember the lessons of humanity taught to you by your elders.

We will be known forever by the tracks we leave

In other people's lives, our kindness and generosity

Take the time to walk a mile in his moccasins."

- By Mary T. Lathrap (1895)

Well, let's begin with something that I think we all know about and something that we have all experienced. *Sympathy.*

Sympathy is the ability — for want of a better way to phrase this — to feel sorry for someone. Let's consider a homeless person. Very sadly in the year that this book was published (2023) homelessness has spiralled.

Government statistics from the ONS (Office of National Statistics) says that right now homeless is nearly 20% higher than it was at the same time of the previous year. We think that there are nearly 29,000 homeless people in this country. In every town and city you will see the evidence. Sleeping bags in doorways. People begging for money on the streets. Tents pitched in unusual places for long periods of time.

Homelessness is a brutal experience for anyone. For someone who is homeless the effects are *horrific* — their mental health with suffer, their physical health will suffer, they will probably struggle to clean their clothes, they will struggle to wash and eat a healthy diet. They will be treated disrespectfully by lots of people. They become dehumanised and seen as a problem.

At some stage that homeless person was a child at school. They didn't grow up aiming to live on the streets. Whatever happened in their lives — whatever choices they made and whatever went wrong for them — here they now live.

When you walk down the street and you pass a homeless person who is asking you for change – do you acknowledge them as a human being? Do you apologise and say "I'm sorry" if you don't have anything to give?

Many, many people don't. It's actually sad how many people don't.

When you see a homeless person on the street and you can see they have been struggling and that they are in hardship – you might feel bad for them, maybe a bit grateful that you're not in that position too – but mainly you just feel bad for them: *that's what we call sympathy*.

Something strikes a chord in you and you feel it inside and no matter what you might show outside, inside you're thinking "That poor individual". You might just wish that it wasn't happening. You might not know what to do, you might not do anything about it – but inside you experience an emotion. That emotion is tinged with pain, it's a sadness – you do not think that it is fair. There might even be a touch of anger in that sadness. You're not angry at them, you see them as a victim of their circumstances, and you just pass through that emotion.

It might stay with you all day. It might pass by in a minute. *That is sympathy*. It's like being on a train that passes through a station that it doesn't stop at. The train rattles through. The carriages reverberate. You feel the fact that you moved through there. You hear the noise. The light through the window flickers. The train-tracks rattle a little bit differently and just for a moment you realise how fast you are travelling. Just like that you're through and out of the other side and you keep on going – but you never stop.

Sympathy is very much like that because despite your sympathy – you don't do anything – you just feel it and you keep on moving.

Here is a sympathy statement:

"I feel bad for you I really do, and I wish there was something that I could do but there just isn't."

That is a sympathetic statement.

You might say "What good does that do anyone?" or "That is absolutely no use at all". Ok – I get you. I see what you're saying there. However, you need to think about the people who walk on by and feel nothing for the homeless. *At least a sympathetic person is acknowledging the existence of someone else in the same shared world?* At least that sympathy that comes up inside of that someone shares the pain for just a second and verifies what is there – that what is happening there on the street – is not ok? It might not be very much better – but I would take that over someone who walks on by and feels nothing – every single day of the week.

Now you might think that the next thing you're going to move to, from sympathy, is doing something positive to make a change to that problem. That would be logical.

Actually, the next complex emotion you are likely to experience before you get to that stage is 'empathy'.

Rather than jumping to the place where you 'do something', you are likely to move into a place where you start to imagine what it is like to be in that problem yourself.

Instead of seeing it as something that is unique to the person who is suffering – you allow yourself to admit that this could happen to anyone. If this could happen to anyone – this could happen to me. What would I do? What would that be like? For me? Empathy can be a scary thing to experience. It's more reassuring to tell yourself that it could never happen to you.

So, with homelessness you might start to contemplate your day. Waking up cold in a doorway – maybe with someone telling you that you have to move on. You need to go to the toilet but you have nowhere to go in privacy and use an actual toilet. If you do go off to a public toilet – what is going to happen to your stuff while you are gone? Will it be there when you get back? If it got stolen or removed, and you lost your sleeping bag, where on earth would you sleep? You realise that you smell pretty bad – you'd like to get a shower – where can you do that? Do you have any toiletries? What about food? What about breakfast?

This problem of being on the street starts to surround you and you appreciate just how bad it is.

You're beginning to walk the first steps of a mile in the shoes of this homeless person. Oh my goodness – you thought that sympathy was a painful emotion. Empathy? Empathy is like the difference between something in two dimensions, and something in virtual reality. Empathy surrounds you, it crowds you – if you actually do commit to thinking this through it opens you up to all kinds of thoughts and feelings.

Suddenly you begin to realise the value of things. My goodness. What a realisation!

In the previous chapter we talked about our teachers – we talked about Miss Peterson being verbally abused in her lesson by someone who didn't do their homework. Walk that situation through in your head. How would it feel to be that teacher in that situation? Not as Miss Peterson – but as you?

You can do this with your peers – when you form the bonds of friendship, and you really feel like you have that loyalty to a good friend. You have that empathy with them because you know that they see the world this way for you, and you see the world that way for them too. Their welfare and their wellbeing become as important to you as it is to them. We all have people in our lives that we feel this way about – and we can't, and we shouldn't feel this way about everyone (we couldn't possibly cope with that – we couldn't function) but it's a huge jump forward. We stop doing things just for ourselves and our own gain – and we start to care about the welfare of others. We begin to realise that if we endure a little hardship, discomfort, or inconvenience – it might actually make the world an awful lot better, much, much better – for someone else.

So, empathy leads us to motivation – it changes how we behave. It leads us to a new place and this new place is called 'compassion'.

'Compassion' is about using your empathy – and then making a decision to improve things for that other person or a group of people. Improving things for them. Improving things for you. Improving things for everyone.

Where sympathy says *"I would really like to help you – I just can't do anything about that"*, empathy makes that unacceptable and compassion says "I can see what you're going through – I don't know what we can do with this – but there must be something".

After seeing that person living on the streets you might sit on the bus and google 'solutions to homelessness' or 'how do I help the homeless'?

You might sit and think about what you **can** do and the difference you **can** make to that particular problem. After a while you are going to realise that you don't need to be Elon Musk or Jeff Bezos, with limitless amounts of money, to address homelessness as a problem (problems are rarely solved just by throwing money at them).

Ok so you're not a billionaire, you can't just buy people somewhere to live, but you sit and you think about it. You realise, you could write to the council and express your concerns. You could volunteer at a foodbank or at a meal kitchen. You could collect literature about health services and support and take it down to all the homeless people.

You could donate clothes and other items to a homelessness charity. You could setup a small direct debit that takes a little donation out of your account every month and gives it to a registered charity. You might go even further and start to organise other people and mobilise a local response in your community. Perhaps you come up with a great idea, and you decide to apply for a grant, you start to put the pieces together in your spare time. All of a sudden you realise that it's completely ridiculous to think "I just can't do *anything*" you realise how powerful you are! In fact, you can do lots of things, when you challenge yourself.

Sometimes it takes a huge amount of personal honesty to say to yourself "I don't like that situation – but if I'm being really honest, I can't be *bothered* to do anything" but it is rare for people to go through empathy and then do absolutely *nothing* as a consequence.

Empathy is a complicated emotion and it can lead you into things that you'd frankly prefer not to get dragged into. When you start to care, you look down the road and you realise that doing something – actually making a change – is probably going to be tiresome, hard work, not much fun. With a deep sigh you might realise that empathy – and listening to you your conscience[7] – means that you can't turn your back on doing something. It would be easier to do nothing – it is *always* easier to do *nothing*. This is going to cost you time and effort now.

---

[7] The inner voice that tells you right from wrong.

Oh great!

You also know that you're not going to feel good if you do nothing at all.

After you've done something positive – you will feel better – you will be glad that you did it, but in that initial moment, you might feel *reluctant*.

Of course, you don't want people to sleep on the streets at night. Nobody does. Applying empathy and showing some compassion – even if it just means that you buy someone a hot cup of coffee – that's not particularly that hard in that situation to do something small to help.

Let me give you another situation which will test your empathy in a more complicated way. Empathy is *not* easy. It gets actually gets really difficult – but never more so than when you feel that someone has wronged you or disrespected you! You start to feel conflicting emotions.

Maybe it is a situation where you are watching someone do something that you fundamentally disagree with. That can make you quite judgemental.

Alternatively, it could be a situation where you are competing against someone. That's really hard. To remain compassionate – to show empathy – when someone is competing against you for something that you want so badly?

How do stay true to what we have just said?

It gets messy. Your ability to do that is a mark of your maturity and if you can do it well, people will never forget you for it. People will respect you and admire you for it. Universally it is an *honourable* trait.

Being able to rise above your most primary instincts – to claim your revenge, to win at all costs, to get your own back – that is an incredible act of self-control, and it displays wisdom that speaks about who you are as a person.

We need an example here. So I'm going to tell you a short story. In doing so I want to reference round-the-world yachts-person, Pete Goss. His book **'Close to the Wind'**[8] tells you all the details about what happened in the Vendee Globe 1996/7 event and it's an amazing thing to read.

I want you to understand something: more astronauts have circled the Earth than yachts-people have sailed solo around the world non-stop without assistance. What Pete Goss was

---

[8] Headline Book Publishing (1998)

trying to do was staggeringly ambitious. He is a former Royal Marine commando. His determination, his preparation and his focus were incredible.

Pete Goss was racing to accomplish his life's goal. He was going to sail single handed around the globe faster than anyone ever had... but as he sailed for victory through a terrible storm, he learned that his closest competitor had met with a terrible accident. Frenchman, Raphael Dinelli, had his boat wrecked in hurricane force winds as he chased Goss through the hostile Southern Ocean.

Learning the news via a fax transmission (the technology of the day!), Goss turned his boat around, abandoned his dream, and sailed back to look for the wreckage and to rescue Dinelli from certain death. He searched for Dinelli for two whole days.

Today Goss and Dinelli are the closest of friends and Goss was the best-man at Dinelli's wedding. They went on to sail together and win together. Goss could have convinced himself that someone else would go to the aid of Dinelli, or that he couldn't possibly save his competitor – he chose more than sympathy. He turned his boat around and sailed back into a hurricane to rescue the man who had set out to try to stop Goss from achieving everything that he wanted in his life.

When Goss brought Dinelli back home alive he was celebrated everywhere. He was awarded an MBE by HM

Queen Elizabeth II, and the Legion d'Honneur in France by the French President, Jacques Chirac.

Goss could have been the fasted man to sail solo around the globe, but Dinelli would almost certainly have died as a consequence. Goss abandoned the work of a lifetime – blood, sweat and tears. Everything that had brought him to that point.

In secondary school you will experience lots of things that test your ability to see the world from the perspective of other people, or might require you to do the right thing by not putting yourself first all the time. That ability to see the bigger picture and to compromise and reflect, is going to be a huge asset to you.

Sympathy is where you see a situation and you know it's not good. You feel sorry for the person.

Empathy is when you start to see it from their point of view and imagine yourself in that situation.

Compassion is when you decide to help and do something about it.

Learning how to Empathise –

Checklist:

- Sympathy is feeling bad when you see someone in a difficult situation.

- Empathy is taking a further step to imagine what it would be like if it was happening to you.

- Compassion is doing something (no matter how small) to make the situation better.

- Sometimes we forget to recognise the challenges and goals of other people.

- It can help you to talk to other people about things that you've seen that caused you to feel sympathy.

- Being compassionate doesn't mean you have to abandon your goals, but there are times when you also have to accept that your goals aren't as immediately important.

Chapter 3:
What do you want to become?

It's an interesting question. It might not feel like it's very real. You've been in education and school so long that it probably feels like this is what you are and what you're going to do for the rest of your life – even if you hate it! Being at school is very strange because it kind of defines you and who you are. Young people used to be noted as 'school boys' or 'school girls' and effectively, one year to the next – that's exactly what you were and what you did.

That feeling of trudging on from one educational year to the next might seem like it is never going to end, particularly because it's all you've ever known. Also when you look ahead five years you might think that five years is forever – after all, five years ago you might have only been six, seven or eight years old! *That's nearly half your whole life again!!*

In reality though – the time is going to start *accelerating*. Every year feels a little bit shorter as it goes by. Before you know it, you're in Year 9 making options choices on your GCSE subjects. After that, and it seems quite sudden, you find yourself in your final year and you look around thinking *"How on earth did this happen?"*.

Some people feel dizzy and at the end of it all they say "Nobody warned me…"

That's a fair warning!

The difficulty in the UK school system is that we ask people to make very important choices quite early on. By comparison, in the United States the education system stays very broad right up until the point where people go to University (or 'College' as they call it). Even then people don't decide what they 'major' in (i.e. what the topic of their degree will be) until quite late on in their programme.

Here in the UK we start refining our choices at GCSE (14 years old) and it gets more refined again at A Level or college (16) and by the time you go to University (if that is what you want to do) you know what you're going to graduate from before you even arrive at your chosen institution.

It can be bewildering[9] – but more so if you don't know what you want. The people who really succeed have a working idea of what they're aiming for (no matter what that might

---

[9] Confusing and distressing

be) from an early stage. The point of their education is to get towards that goal. Having a goal and an aspiration is important – *beyond important* – and getting what you want is not a cake walk. You have to make sacrifices and do some hard work to get anywhere. *Remember – there are always other people who want the same dream and they might be willing to work harder than you.*

A great piece of wisdom that I really love is:

"Hard work beats talent, when talent doesn't work hard[10]"

It doesn't matter how much natural talent or ability you have – if you don't combine that with hard work (and yes, some sacrifice) the best you can hope to be is a gifted or promising amateur.

By the way, there is nothing more common than someone who doesn't make the most of their promise or their potential. Every teacher has taught hundreds – even thousands of young people - who come under that heading.

Professionals in every field are professionals because of the time and effort they invested. Learning, practising and getting good at *anything* is going to be difficult and sometimes even boring. You have to look up at your dream or your goal and let it inspire you to keep going. If you don't have that dream or goal you will find it ten times harder to motivate yourself through the most difficult pieces of your education. The really outstanding achievement is made by

---

[10] Tim Notke is a High School basketball coach who created this amazing phrase.

people who can work through things they *don't enjoy*, as much as the things that they do.

I work with young people who sit in front of me – and in the most honest way you could possibly imagine - they say "I hate this subject, but more than anything else *I just don't care*". They're being honest with me, and I appreciate that. They cannot stand equations or trigonometry – and I get that! They don't enjoy Shakespeare or Keates - *I didn't like some of that stuff either*! I'm not going to lie to you. I wasn't great at maths and I wasn't a highly motivated student of maths… BUT I got the grade that I needed to progress (it wasn't an A or a 9 by the way). I knew that I wanted to go to university (you might not want that, you might want something else of course) and I found out what that meant for me in maths. I needed – in old money – a grade C at GCSE (or a 4 or 5 in modern GCSE grading). Do you know what? *I got a C* – I got that grade 5. Have I ever faced questions about that? *No* – because it was what I needed, no more and no less. If I hadn't got a grade C (5) it would have called into question my basic level of numeracy (my ability to count and to operate with sums at a pretty basic level).

Let's remind ourself what GCSEs are by the way:

'General Certificate of Secondary Education'

It's the piece of paper you leave school with that says whether you have the entry level skills against a variety of different topics. The core topics are maths, English and the

sciences. If you go for an apprenticeship you can bet your last pound that you'll be asked about *maths, English and science*. If you go for A levels – maths, English and science. If you apply for a job – maths, English and science. <u>That is just how it is.</u>

So let's go back to what *you* want to be – what you want to become in your life.

Now let's say that you want to be an engineer. You realise late on that you'd really like to get into engineering – building bridges or railways or designing machinery or even computer software. Maths - you decided early on that it didn't make sense, you hated it and you just didn't care.

Now maths is starting to make a little sense, and you realise that actually, you'd like to be an engineer. You have always been a practical person and you like solving problems. You'd love to get an engineering apprenticeship… problem: *you kind of gave up on maths back down the line and now you're predicted a 2 or a 3*. Suddenly you *do care* and it does matter and you're angry at yourself and the system for the situation that you've found yourself in.

<u>Let's avoid this potential situation</u> – we need to invest some time and thought in finding out what it is that you want to do as soon as possible.

I am willing to bet that if there is something out there that excites you and that you enjoy – there is a job for that.

Skiing instructor?

Marine biologist researching the preservation of dolphins?

Sports psychologist?

Physiotherapist?

Academic in literature?

Writer?

You might like the idea of working in elite sports – but you feel that you don't have the talent or the physical gifts to be an elite sports person. That's ok – *few people do* – but the elite sports industry is built upon the hard work of people around those athletes. From equipment designers, to coaches, to psychologists, to dieticians, to personal representatives and agents...

If you are lucky enough to meet someone at the very top of their industry *they will all have something in common*. They will have a team of people around them who make it possible. When people win awards what do they always say?

"I wouldn't be here today if it wasn't for the practical support and the belief of..."

Have you ever watched a boxing fight? At the end of every three minute round that fighter goes back to his or her corner, sits down on a stool, and they have a person to tend to the cuts, a coach to give advice, someone who cools them down with a sponge.

Watch an awards ceremony where a film star wins a big award. They stand up in front of everyone – they accept the award. They make a speech. Do they say *"I'd like to thank myself because I did this all on my own?"*.

They stand up and they acknowledge the people in their team that made it possible – without whom the 'big star' wouldn't be on top of the world. The people in these teams are well paid experts in their field – sought after by other people – respected in their industry (and well paid). The modern world has a preoccupation with stardom and the spotlight – but you don't have to be a star, and you don't have to be the person in the spotlight to have an exciting career and be a successful person in your own right.

You might not know who Emmanuel Steward was. He was one of the most successful boxing trainers in the world. Ever. Along the way he trained countless athletes and 41 world champions, from Tyson Fury, to Lennox Lewis, Evander Holyfield to Wladimir Klitschko – champions. 41 world champions!

The truth is that there is a world of exciting options out there and for you it begins with enough self-awareness to know what *motivates* you, what is *rewarding* for you, and what you will *enjoy* doing. Do you like working with children? Do you like working with exotic animals? Maybe you like logic and the certainty of maths? It could be that you love music and making music.

There will be a temptation to simply find out who makes the most money.

"Tell me about a career that is well paid"

"Well, hedge-fund managers make lots of money"

"What do they do?"

"They manage investment funds for businesses, pension groups and private individuals. They track the movement of the markets and they invest the money to gain returns, making decisions on how risky such investments are"

"Ok that sounds pretty dull to me" [it might not – that might sound perfect for you by the way]

"They get paid millions of pounds every year"

"Ok – well I'll do that then"

I mean, sure, if the money means that much to you there are a number of ways to find out how to get paid. It's not wrong to be motivated by money either. I would just advise you to try and find something well paid in an industry that isn't something you hate or strongly disagree with. *The tobacco industry makes huge sums of money – billions in fact – but it has also been responsible for millions of recorded deaths.*

You also need to remember this: there will be someone in any industry that is money motivated *and* they love that work genuinely. You'll have to compete with that and their natural enthusiasm to do things that you might not want to do. If you can't love what you do, they'll have that huge advantage over you.

On the other hand, *if you're the very best at what you do*, pretty much no matter what it is, you'll get paid. People always want to hire the best people, those skills are always in demand, and companies always pay extra to get the best. Ok there is a ceiling on what you can earn in certain sectors and certain professions, but if you're the *best* that there is, and you are determined to be the very best in that industry, you will get paid at the highest level available *and* you'll be deeply satisfied.

My advice is to tackle this question early. You have to tackle it sooner or later anyway! So go early. Know what you want, or have a short list of the things that you would like to do. This will give you a natural sense of purpose which leads to momentum[11].

Invariably the people that I find drifting in education are the people who do not know what they want. That is a downward spiral too. If you don't know what you want, you start to fall into a decline. You're unmotivated, and you become stagnant. You're not achieving, and you stop believing in yourself. Suddenly your self-esteem suffers. You start aiming low with things. You might feel jealous of other people who are more successful or seem to have more purpose. You start telling yourself that you could 'never' do things. *"I could never do that"*.

"Yeah it would be cool to be an executive for Disney Corporation and work in the USA – but I could never do that".

---

[11] Energy that helps you to travel forwards.

Someone said (lots of people from Virgil[12] to Henry Ford have said versions of this):

> *"Whatever you decide you can or cannot do – it is usually true".*

Meanwhile – as you drift – you might get a wake-up call. A kid you used to know at primary school just won an award, or got put up in an ability set above you, or outscored you in a test... and you used to be doing better than that kid. You used to regularly outperform that kid in primary school. Now look at him or her kicking your backside! The funny thing is – he/she doesn't even realise that they're doing it, either. It doesn't matter to them that they're doing better than you at that thing because *you don't figure in what they're doing*. They have their sights on other things – a goal. *You don't.*

As you drift, they come swimming past you. **Working harder and with more purpose.**

Now this isn't a competition. It really isn't – but you can't help but compare yourself to others. It's what we call 'a benchmark'. You look at where they are, where they were – and you compare your own progress. You naturally want to know where you sit overall in the class. It's a way of having a sense of your progress. **I have never met anyone who couldn't do better if they tried harder.**

Michael Jordan went to play 'college' basketball before he went to the Chicago Bulls. He played for University of North

---

[12] A great ancient Roman poet and writer. Thought to have died 19 years before Jesus was born.

Carolina. When he met his coach he told him "I want to be the best player that ever played for this college". His coach looked at him with surprise and said *"Well you're going to have to work harder!"*. Jordan said "What do you mean?! I work as hard as everyone else!" The coach replied *"Well I thought you wanted to be better than everyone else?"*

What Michael Jordan had (in addition to his natural talent and ability for the game of basketball) – was a *determination to win*. He knew what his goal was from an early stage, and he stuck to that and he worked hard for it every single day without compromise. He protected that dream, and he went after it in every single way that he could.

It really does not matter what your dream or goal is – if you apply the same level of determination there is nobody there to stop you. In truth, the only person you compete with is actually… you.

How do I find the thing that I really want to become?

For a lot of people it begins with not being overawed by the possibilities. I mean – even with a certain degree of realism in the mix (let's say that you're 13 years old and you never played tennis – but all of a sudden you fancy winning Wimbledon – honestly this is unlikely) – the range of opportunities is scary. It genuinely is.

[As a contrast to that – Jimi Hendrix, the rock-and-roll hall of fame guitar genius, didn't start playing until he was 13, he

only played for 14 years and tragically died when he was 27 – so we should never say never.]

One thing that I encounter time and time again is that girls who lack a sense of direction, purpose and motivation get pointed towards a 'hair and beauty' course at a local college. Maybe it's thought to be an 'easy' option? The boys – by comparison – get pointed towards some type of trade apprenticeship (carpentry, bricklaying, becoming an electrician). *I do not know why this sexism persists.* Every single girl out there could be just as good as an electrician or a builder. There are lots of guys who would excel in women's hair and beauty. Some of the most famous hair stylists are guys. Vidal Sassoon was a legend in creating iconic women's hair styles – some of the looks that he created defined the fashions of the 1960s.

I get positively angry when I hear these fallback positions because most of them are lazy ways to avoid having to solve one of the most important and exciting problems any person will encounter in their whole life. Most of the time when I have that conversation with a young person they say "The pay is ok and I guess it'll do". They shrug. Their parents approve.

Wow – at 14 years old – and we're already settling for 'It'll do'.

I was on holiday in Norway in the city of Bergen. I encountered a lady who was a photographer. She had a studio and I walked in there to look at her pictures. She had incredible photos of Native Americans playing musical instruments. This might make you think of traditional Native American music – but she deliberately sought to break that image by photographing Native Americans playing electric guitars, drums, trumpets, pianos and other instruments. Her work recast the image of the Native American as a separated race held on a reservation. It was simple and thought provoking. The nature of the photography was beautiful and brought an emotional response out of you for looking at it. In short, her work was brilliant.

I asked the photographer how she got into the industry and she told me that she had a camera as a child and she loved it – she loved taking photos and capturing images, constructing images, developing and producing her own pictures – and it grew from there. I also asked her who had told her that she could do this professionally?

"Nobody."

I told her that I thought she was very brave because she had decided to do this for a living and that she had done something as incredible as travelling to America seeking these images and believing that they were waiting for her out there. She told me something that really changed a lot of things for me and made me reflect on myself – I thought it was very wise:

"I didn't feel that I had a choice – deep down this is who I am – and I only chose to be true to myself".

Well – that short statement really made me think.

In the choices that I had made for my life – how many of them were as uncompromising as that? When had I drawn a line and decided "This is who I am – so this is what I'm going to do". I cannot honestly say that I had ever done such a thing. There was an empowerment to what that lady was doing and it wasn't about the fact that she was a professional photographer or artist. It really could have been anything – that is, anything that was an honest reflection of what was inside of her and how she chose to define herself.

It is definitely worth realising that when you choose a career, it really does speak about who you are and what your values are. This is possibly your first chance in life to do that. There is a lot of pressure on you to make the right choice – and perhaps you feel that your parents are watching you carefully in the hope that you'll say something that society respects a great deal and has a huge amount of social status attached to it. The classic choices of this nature are 'doctor' or 'lawyer' – some cultures and backgrounds make jokes that the traditional 'pushy parents' are always nudging their children towards medical school or law school.

It takes a lot to stand up to the world and say "I'm going to be a dancer" – the inherent insecurity of the industry makes it a terrifying choice and only the best of the best are paid.

Maybe you want to stand up and say "I'm going to be an artist" – a profession traditionally associated with very low pay and difficult personal sacrifices (unless you become a huge and very fashionable figure for some reason – an Andy Warhol).

These are all reasons why it is so much easier to stay in the herd with everyone else and just meekly say "I'm going to do hair and beauty" or "I'm going to be a carpet fitter" – when really you want to dance!

If you want to be successful in school, I recommend that you define what *your success* is going to look like. Your success is entirely dependent on what outcomes you really need and want.

"I want to be a photographer" means very different things compared to "I want to be an astrophysicist". Your outcomes and your needs change in a fundamental way. Believe in this though – *and believe it very strongly* – you are the person who has to live with your outcomes and nobody else. The outcomes you seek should be the ones you need – not the ones that impress someone else or make other people think you're sensible. They don't live with your consequences – you do.

Jimi Hendrix was a visionary and a musical genius. He played the guitar in a way that was different to anyone who came before him, and possibly since. To hear recordings of how Jimi Hendrix played the guitar is unmistakable – it can only be Jimi Hendrix. Sometimes when he played people said that it didn't sound 'right'. He dressed in a way that nobody had seen before – his colour choices, his hats, old military jackets, waist coats, swirling patterns and ladies belts and accessories... He said:

"I'm the one that's got to die when it's time for me to die, so let me live my life the way I want to."

For me he pretty much nailed it there. Life is a one-shot deal. You get yours and you get one go at it. Everyone else gets their own – let them get on with it. When the time comes, you die and the time is up. Whatever you did – that's what you achieved in your life. Will you be proud of it and happy?

If you leave a mountain of cash behind you – will that be a suitable testament to your time?

If you have a funeral and hundreds of friends attend and mourn your passing – will that be your achievement?

Remember that finding the thing that you want to become really depends on putting yourself into the future and looking backwards from there. If you can find a position from which looking backwards makes you feel proud and happy – the chances are that you've found the thing that you need to become.

This might be daunting. When you find that thing it might scare you because it seems like a steep climb. At least you know where you're going, how you need to prepare yourself and what you're going to do next.

NB. A final point

I have made points in this chapter about selecting a career in 'hair and beauty' or 'a trade apprenticeship'. Allow me to clarify. These are tremendous careers and we need people who go into these industries – but if you are going in that direction, just make sure that you're doing it because that's what you want to be. Don't do it if it just seems like the easiest route and you're on a conveyor belt that you don't even control. I have no problem with such industries – of course I don't – but I do have a problem with such industries being used as a catch net for people who haven't really tackled the issue of "What should I become?". Whatever you choose – understand that even if you stand still and do nothing at all – you're making a choice. Don't choose out of fear – love the choice you are making and do something that you can really invest your life into.

I'm going to be an astronaut!

Houston! We have a problem!

What do I want to become?

Checklist:

- Life can be as dull or as interesting as you choose to make it.
- Being motivated at school is much easier when you have a sense of purpose in life.
- Find a goal or an aim and it will guide you to know what you need to achieve in school.
- Don't choose from what you think you can get in school. *Challenge yourself to get what you need to fit the goal.* Choose the goal first.
- If you are excellent at anything you will rise to the top and you will be rewarded.
- Being motivated by money is fine – but why not choose something that you are naturally passionate about, and then get paid for that?
- Life is a one-shot deal so don't settle for second best.

Chapter 4:
Dealing with conflict

Dealing with conflict is a big issue. Even if you're reading this thinking "I have no intention of coming into conflict with anyone" – disagreements do happen, and when they happen they can be upsetting. People can fall into disagreement about any range of things and from my experience the most minor things – if handled in a clumsy way – can turn into a big deal and escalate without much warning. Even for people who step carefully, conflict and disagreement is a thing that is likely to happen. Alternatively, you might be on the receiving end of something that you didn't appreciate – and you need to know how to challenge that without it becoming confrontational or resulting in conflict.

'Reductive' means it has been over simplified

Misapprehension

One of the biggest and most chaotic factors – for the modern teenager – is social media. Social media encourages what was call 'reductive thinking' – that is shortening and boiling things down until they become punchy statements that cause a lot of impact, but don't illustrate the full depth of a topic.

Social media encourages you to try to capture your thoughts on quite complicated topics and express them in as few words as possible – often accompanied with an image that expresses something alongside it. The problem with this is that it leaves so much room for interpretation and very often people can make up their own mind about the true meaning that you were trying to express.

Remember that words are just like sign posts bobbing around in the sea. We leave them in places and expect them to stay there, but they float away into odd spaces sometimes until they lose their original significance – or mean different things to different people. Even language itself can be unreliable!

I'll give you a key example:

I was recently informed that the word 'dank' means 'really good'.

Now this is a piece of slang, it is probably quite localised to where I live and work. It might not mean the same for someone in Glasgow or Newcastle and definitely not for someone in a foreign country who is looking up the word for translation.

'Dank', as far as I was concerned, meant 'not very nice'. You might describe a damp basement in an old building as 'dank'. It smells bad, it's mouldy, it's cold... it's 'dank'.

This is a quite traditional reading of the word.

Even in my lifetime I've seen the word 'bad' go from meaning negative, to meaning positive and cool, back to meaning something is negative again.

This is baffling[13].

If we can't even rely on our words to mean what they are supposed to mean, how do we communicate effectively at all?

This is much more of a problem in short bursts of social media or in direct messaging through services like SnapChat and WhatsApp.

In a lengthy conversation you can get, from the pattern of my language, whether I am using the word 'dank' in a modern, localised, streetwise way or whether I am using a traditional version of the word. The same is true of any other word – such as when I say that something is 'bad'. This is called context. When people say that they have been quoted 'out of context' this is what they are saying has happened.

"So I said that Rachel had come out as gay and Mason said that was 'bad' – I was shocked."

---

[13] Just to be clear that means deeply confusing.

In this context it looks like Mason is homophobic – someone who is prejudiced against gay people.

[Actually the word 'homophobia' means having an irrational fear of homosexual people – but again – words float away from their meanings over time]

Anyone who knows Mason knows that he is fond of hip urban 1980s phrases and often refers to people and things as 'bad' when he admires them, thinks they are bold, and generally considers it to be a positive thing.

Overall this is what we call a 'misapprehension'. The word to 'apprehend' means to 'understand' or 'anticipate in a negative way'. These two things tend to come together under the same word when we 'misapprehend' – which is like saying *"What I thought Mason said was that Rachel was a bad person because she was gay, or maybe just because she came out as gay – but either way, I thought Mason was passing comment in a homophobic and unsupportive way that was slurring her identity"*.

So already the statement by Mason is starting to grow and expand in the mind of the person who heard it or received it. They are adding things to the statement that weren't there and that Mason certainly didn't intend.

The 'misapprehension' comes under the same category as 'misunderstanding'. The person has leapt to a conclusion – but perhaps not wanting to challenge Mason directly has then sought the opinion of someone else.

"So I said that Rachel had come out as gay and Mason said that was 'bad' – I was shocked."

"Nah – Mason's not like that, I'm pretty sure you must have heard him wrong"

"No look, it's on my Snap messages – see…"

"Oh wow"

[The message from Mason literally responds with "I always thought that she might be – that's bad!"]

So Mason has no idea that he has sparked this situation or caused any offence or alarm. He is going about his day, meanwhile assisted by social media, e-messaging, and every other piece of technology (including screenshots without context and so on) a drama blows up that he has no idea about.

The people who learn about this whole situation decide to take this stuff back to Rachel – who seeing the messages, and feeling very vulnerable because she's just made a big personal statement to the world around her, interprets the same misapprehension. She was warned by people who are supporting her sincerely *"You'll be really surprised – the people who you least expect to turn on you will do it. There is always someone."*

Thinking about it, Rachel interprets this situation as exactly that. "So Mason is like that." She might get angry, she might become confrontational, she might feel very hurt and upset. This could go in a number of directions. As it turns out, it hurts her enough to make her worry that other people feel the same:

"Oh my gosh – how many friends are going to turn on me like this. I can't take this back. This is out of my control now. I don't know what to say or do."

Rachel thinks about this on her own and ends up in tears. Her big brother is two years older than her and Gary is very protective of his little sister. *"I never liked Mason – leave this to me – I'm going to sort this out!"*.

Ok this situation is going to get very out of hand by the looks of things.

Lots of people now 'know'** that:

a) Rachel has just come out as gay
b) Mason reacted in a homophobic way
c) It really upset Rachel, and Gary is going to 'sort Mason out' for it

**When we say that people 'know' – they think that they know (even if they don't) – and this is now just the understood situation that is unfolding.*

People start taking sides. People make up their minds. You get a range of views and people start chatting about it in person and online:

"Mason is a homophobe. I always knew it. He says things are 'gay' if he doesn't think they're any good. This isn't the first time you know."

"Nah – he's not like that – his cousin is gay and they're really close. People are just misunderstanding this."

"Look at the screen shot – you can't argue with that."

The drama – as it has now become – from one misapprehension, begins to build and unfold. Rachel and Mason have not had any conversation to clarify their feelings at all. Some people pile on, not feeling one way or another – they just like the drama and the excitement. Some people just want to see what will happen when Gary catches up with Mason, and cruelly, they just pour petrol on the flames:

"Hey Gary – you're not gonna let Mason disrespect your sister like that are you?"

Inevitably someone else makes something up that is completely and entirely false – because that's easy to do on social media:

"I heard he said stuff about your Mum too Gary."

"Oh Gary – you can't let him get away with that"

When Gary catches up with Mason he's already super angry and aggressive. He is much bigger and older than Mason, and Mason is scared and intimidated. Remember, Mason didn't actually say anything homophobic – his language was a bit clumsy and unclear – but what he actually meant to say was *"Oh I think that's great – I respect her for doing that"*. That is genuinely what he meant. By now nobody is willing to believe him.

In this moment, Mason finds himself pinned up against a wall by Rachel's angry big brother and this can go one of two ways:

Mason might hurriedly insist that what he said was not homophobic, he didn't mean it to be homophobic, he said that it was 'bad' like *"Oh man she's so brave – that's amazing – I'm glad for her"*.

Well, right now, as he is pinned up against a wall, people are thinking *"Oh yeah Mason – as if – you're just trying to avoid getting beaten up! We saw what you wrote."*

The situation has escalated *really* badly – it's hard for Mason to express what has happened in a way that people will accept to be true. Afterall it is also true that he has used the term 'gay' to suggest that things are weak or not very good in the past – and that's definitely not ok.

Regardless of whether he is guilty or innocent of having expressed homophobia against Rachel – he interprets the challenge from Gary as what we call 'a loss of face'. This is how his second reaction might play out: he is embarrassed, and his pride has been stung. All these people gathering round waiting to see what will happen. If he backs down and apologises in any way, people are going to call him a coward – and they'll think he did something he didn't do anyway.

Mason thinks that he is going to get beaten up anyway. No matter what he says or does right now.

In addition, adrenaline is rushing through him and he is feeling very defensive.

In this situation Mason might do something irrational – that is, something that doesn't make a lot of sense logically. When Gary's attention is drawn to something that someone called out to one side of him, and he looks away briefly, Mason punches Gary in the face. A whole fight breaks out between the two and the whole group of onlookers just gets even bigger. People start rushing to see what is going on. The boys fight harder, hitting each other with more determination.

A teacher intervenes and Gary is physically pushed way from Mason. Gary is furious – red faced *"He said homophobic things about my sister! And he threw the first punch!"*

Mason is red faced and he is angry too *"I was just walking along and this animal grabbed me and started accusing me of things!"*.

In their anger both boys claim they acted in self-defence – but on another level, they both know that at least for a moment in time, they lost their tempers and they wanted to hurt each other.

With the adrenaline, and another natural chemical called cortisone, rushing through their bodies neither boy feels like they have been hurt, and in fact if they were left alone they would probably end up throwing punches at each other again.

It takes time for them to calm down and get some semblance of sensible thought back. When they do, they realised that they are hurt. Mason has a split lip and cut above his eye. He first realises this when he notices there is blood on his school shirt. Gary has a black eye and is already telling his friend *"He sucker punched me when I looked away"*.

The more they calm down the more these injuries sting and hurt. Their hands begin to swell and hurt a lot.

Mason slowly realises that he has a pain in his side, and it turns out that he has a broken rib. This was a nasty incident. Breaking a rib is surprisingly easy to do and it happens in contact sports like rugby and boxing a lot. There is nothing that anyone can do – it has to heal up on its own – but it's very painful.

The crowd of onlookers, also now full of adrenaline and caught up in it all, gleefully talk about who 'won' the fight. The talk of a 'rematch' is now spreading. Someone suggests, falsely, that Gary has already promised to jump Mason and both boys shouted things at each other in the heat of the moment that neither really meant – they were just being insulting and they were trying to vent their anger.

We are now looking at a situation turning into 'beef' or a 'feud' – and while Gary will always claim it is about defending his sister from abuse, he now feels personally invested in showing everyone that if the teachers hadn't intervened he would have 'won' the fight. Additionally,

Gary, two years older and much bigger, is walking around with a big black eye that he got from a much smaller and younger boy. Gary's peers in his own year enjoy winding him up about that.

"Nice one Gary – who did you fight? Mike Tyson? Tyson Fury? Ha ha!"

For a lot of people this situation looks like it cannot be recovered. Left on its own it might go from bad to worse. Neither Gary nor Mason have the skills to resolve this without further problems, more confrontation or possibly violence. Both boys have already got themselves suspended from school for violent misconduct.

Let's take the opportunity to break this situation down into pieces and look at what the options were at different stages as it unfolded. *How could this have been prevented?* How could this have been avoided? What can we do with this situation now to make it better?

Let's break this into stages:

Stage 1 — Where the initial misapprehension happens. Mason replies to the original person he was messaging with about Rachel. He made his comment and it gave rise to the original misunderstanding. At this stage it really is just about a misunderstanding between himself and that person. *Should they have been talking about Rachel?*

Stage 2　The person who initially received the message from Mason is surprised by his response and is perhaps distressed or unhappy. *Could this person have simply clarified the message to avoid misapprehension?*

Stage 3　The person who initially received the message chose to share it more broadly. *Did this help?*

Stage 4　Rachel found out and she was genuinely hurt.

Stage 5　Rachel's brother finds out and becomes angry – did he need to? Did it help Rachel?

Stage 6　The confrontation.

Stage 7　The after event of the confrontation.

This is what we call 'escalation' – and by that we consider 'how the situation got so bad'.

At stage 1 this situation is between Mason and one other person. Mason intends no ill towards anyone – he's a genuinely nice guy even if his previous language about things being 'gay' (when he doesn't like them) is clumsy and inappropriate. He's not malicious[14]. Mason needs to be more careful about his language. In the first instance saying things are 'gay' (if you mean that they are embarrassing, substandard or not good) is a genuinely homophobic misuse of language. If you do this without thinking about it you are being homophobic and you are slurring gay people. *It is not ok.* Sadly Mason has set a context which is common and needs to be challenge – it is evidence of a form of toxic

> 'Hetero-normative' means treating gay people as if they're not normal.

masculine behaviour [15] – it suggests that heterosexual behaviour is 'normal' and homosexual behaviour is

---

[14] Malicious means intending anyone harm or upset.
[15] Toxic masculine behaviour is when a boy tries to behave as you would expect a strong, dominant man would – but in an unhealthy or a harmful way e.g. resorting to violence.

'abnormal' or 'defective'. This is what we call 'heteronormative behaviour'. By not challenging this use of language, and indeed by using this language casually 'because other people do it' Mason has set himself up to make people ask "Does Mason have a problem with gay people?" or "Does Mason have a problem with people being gay?". *This opens the door for the larger problems that we encounter later as things develop.*

So Mason uses a phrase that is 'ambiguous' – that is, it could mean two or more things. It could mean that he's unhappy to learn that Rachel is gay OR it could mean that he thinks that her decision to tell people that she is gay is brave and he totally respects her for doing it. *It really could mean either thing.*

The person he is messaging could simply say "What do you mean – are you unhappy with Rachel?" and he would obviously respond "No no, I mean it's a badass thing to stand up for yourself and be that courageous".

[At this point I do wish to clarify for myself that I don't think that it ought to be a courageous thing to tell people that you're gay – I hope for a world where it really doesn't matter to anyone and people can co-exist without having anxiety over this topic – but I acknowledge that if you're about 13 or 14 years old and you want to be open about your sexuality, I think that is likely to make you feel anxious and insecure. If you do it anyway - that's brave.]

A simple clarification would have probably prevented anything from developing. It's a shared responsibility – Mason needs to work on his use of language so that his words express more clearly what he is thinking and feeling (and we all have that responsibility). The other person could also take responsibility for being more upfront in that situation and asking a mature question that doesn't inflame the situation or jump to conclusions. Stopping something from escalating or becoming something that it doesn't need to be can be as simple as that.

If anyone has ever watched a video of how a fire spreads they'll understand that it doesn't begin with huge fire – it starts with ignition, a spark, a small flame and it moves from there. Recognising the danger and stopping the spread before it becomes too big to manage is important.

Any fire needs three things to grow – heat, oxygen and fuel. If you combine those three things there *will* be a fire.

Now we are in stage 2. Rather than clarifying the situation with Mason the person who received the message dwells on it, grows uncomfortable about it, makes up their own mind about it – perhaps they feel too awkward to go back to Mason about it... *they start thinking the worst and they go to the worst possible outcome.*

We all do this from time to time – we do this about ourselves, we do this about other people – our natural ability to think the worst, assume the worst, comes out. Sometimes we have to control this instinct. We have talked about sympathy, empathy and compassion earlier on in this book. It feels bad when people assume the worst about us — it would feel pretty bad to be Mason and having to consider *"He/she really thinks that I'm homophobic — they think that's what I'm like"*. So maybe Stage 2 is still an opportunity for that person to go back to Mason — but likewise — as we move into Stage 3 there is an opportunity for a friends to show some maturity and say *"Hey, let's talk to Mason in a friendly way about that and we'll find out"*. Additionally, I'd add that Stage 2 is a place where that person has to be honest with themselves. Did they think "Hey I've got some gossip here and this is going to make me popular"? *This happens a lot.* They excitedly rush out and tell someone else just to share a scandal and see their reaction... *how often does gossip become the fuel that makes the fire spread? The attention then becomes the oxygen...*

So we move into stage 3. You have to be *very* careful who you share your private business with because sometimes the people you trust can let you down. "Ok — don't tell anyone this but I have a crush on...". The next thing you know, everyone else knows, *including the person you have the crush on* (I think a lot of people have been in this embarrassing situation). The person you told then 'only told one or two other people who they trusted'. Well guess what? *So did they*, and so did they, and so did they. Ok and guess what else? When they said that they only told 'two other people' — well, maybe it was four, and maybe it happened in the lunchroom... Look, even back in the day when I was at school, and we didn't have any social media (or in fact the internet at all) – rumours still spread *very* quickly. You could go from nobody knowing who you had a crush on in the morning to the world knowing your business by 3PM and the final bell of the day. You wouldn't be surprised to see it on the 6 O'clock news!

6'O Clock News Exclusive

A teenage boy had his crush revealed today...

One thing that happens in the rumour mill is that each person adds a little bit on to it too. It goes from "I don't know if Mason meant it this way but..." to "Well you know that Mason abused Rachel in this chat behind her back". Someone gets hold of it who doesn't know or care about Mason, Rachel, or anyone else involved. They just love the drama and their empathy skills are very low, they demonstrate a lack of maturity about the situation. They spread the gossip. They add oxygen and heat to the fire.

Inevitably then, we get to stage 4. Rachel finds out. She might see a screen shot of the individual comment, she is hearing the comments and the things that people are saying. Suddenly the situation is not just about her, it's about how Mason has reacted to her identity. She is already feeling quite raw and vulnerable anyway – this is a difficult time for Rachel. Has anyone empathised with her about that? Is she getting the support that she needs during this time? Are her friends being true friends? Without that support Rachel is going to end up reaching the wrong conclusion – and that's what happened. Being fair to Rachel I can see why and how that was the result – but again – objectively[16] speaking, honest and mature communication between Mason and Rachel could have made a huge difference. At the same time, maybe she is scared that he will genuinely be unkind to her, he might even say something worse *"Yeah I said it – gay people disgust me..."*. Somehow Rachel needs to clarify what is going on and is confused. More people are talking about her now that she ever thought possible. Mason could still be oblivious to what is happening at this point – or might simply feel scared to reach out. At this point in time there is a lot of heat, oxygen and fuel on this fire and it's getting out of control.

Someone needs to be a friend to Rachel and stop investing in the drama.

The emotions of the situation are driving what is happening - rather than a logical process of thought. Rachel feels

---

[16] Looking at it from more than one perspective.

vulnerable and her instinct is to protect herself, which most people can understand. Rachel needs reassurance, not only that Mason isn't judging her or being homophobic, but more widely that people aren't behaving that way either. Rachel thinks *"If Mason is saying that – how many other people are thinking it without saying it? At least I know Mason is homophobic. Who else is like that and I don't know about it?"*.

Rachel needs reassurance, but a good friend to Rachel would also recognise that and help her to find that reassurance too and maybe resolve this whole situation.

[While this illustration is about a girl coming out – it could be any range of emotionally significant topics and when we talk about being aware of mental and emotional health, this is what mental and emotional health awareness looks like]

Stage 5 happens. So Rachel's big brother Gary finds out and a number of things kick into play. The toxic masculine expectations all fall down on Gary.

"Am I expected to kick this guy's ass for this? Yeah, I think I probably am."

This is literally (and very sadly) the big brother stereotype of 'sticking up for your little sister'. Additionally, Gary cares a lot about his sister. It upsets him to see her so upset. He reacts emotionally too. He isn't detached enough to show what we called 'objectivity'. 'Objectivity' is the opposite of 'subjectivity'. *Subjective* behaviour is about how *he* feels as an individual – it is very specific and only from his point of view. 'Objectivity' is about how lots of people might feel in their different opinions, seeing this situation from a number of points of view, considering many factors in a calm way. *Objectivity* is more likely to help you to see things *how they are* – rather than subjectivity, which is about how you instinctively 'think' or 'suspect' they are. Gary himself is only about 16 years old – so he has his own temper to work on too. Nobody is perfect. Let's be honest, while Gary wants what is best for his little sister, his reaction wasn't the best one he could have chosen (by a long way).

Gary's focus in this situation was on Mason. The person he thinks has upset his little sister (in reality most of this is about the gossip and the chatter that has caused unnecessary hurt to Rachel).

Let's consider a different concept and some advice that the Metropolitan Police in London were issuing around this type of situation.

A young lady dressed in traditional Islamic clothing was subjected to abuse on the London underground. An ignorant and genuinely hateful person made comments about how she should 'go home' and about 'setting off bombs'.

The young lady, naturally, felt targeted and very threatened. The general silence of the other passengers in the busy carriage made her feel embarrassed and that his attitude was being accepted. Someone eventually spoke and told the abuser to shut up *"Keep your dirty language to yourself or I'll punch you in the face"*.

I guess this person was being brave and was standing up for someone else, they were challenging the ignorance of a hate crime and it all came from a well-intentioned place.

The advice from the police is not to target the offender though. *Go to the victim*. Make the victim feel reassured. Either go and sit next to her and reassure her quietly "Don't worry, you're safe, I won't let him hurt you – we don't agree with him" or maybe offer her a seat next to you, or your own seat. By giving her the reassurance, and by showing her that personal warmth you are isolating that offender and in a non-violent way, you are demonstrating that *he* is wrong. Everyone can see where your sympathies are.

For Rachel, what she really needed wasn't an angry violent big brother making it worse – it was for Gary to sit down next to her and talk it through. Give her some emotional support. Listen to her. Help her figure it out.

If you're the big brother figure in someone's life – try to remember that. It's really not your job to go around kicking asses and being violent.

Stage 6 is about the confrontation itself and there is *a lot* going on here. First of all, as this confrontation begins both parties go into what is called 'fight or flight mode'. This is a natural state where our body responds to a threat or a challenge by generating two natural chemicals. Those chemicals are 'adrenaline' (to give you energy and to supercharge your muscular response) and 'cortisone' (a natural but highly effective painkiller) to help you carry on if you get hurt. The cortisone acts so that if you get hurt you won't feel it in that exact moment and you will hopefully be able to get yourself out of danger. These are natural, timeless responses. Our cave people ancestors were having these reactions when they were fighting wild animals thousands of years ago. We have retained them as 'survival instincts'.

While commonly called 'fight or flight' – this generally refers to the instinct that some people have to become aggressive, or alternatively to run away (think scared zebra chased by a hungry lion). There is a third state, which is 'freeze', so perhaps imagine a hedgehog that rolls up into a ball and sits perfectly still until the danger passes.

The highly unfortunate side of this 'fight or flight' mode is that we don't think very clearly or carefully when we are in it. Adrenaline gives us 'tunnel vision' – which on one hand is about the direct focus on the challenge we are confronted by, but on the other hand stops us from thinking around the problem. That's why in this state very simple things like tying a shoelace or using a doorhandle can suddenly become awkward and difficult. We become clumsy and our fine motor skills[17] suffer.

A secondary consequence of cortisone is that you can suffer memory lapses as a result of it – something called 'cortisone amnesia'. As a police officer I used to take statements from people immediately after something had happened to them

---

[17] The skills you use to write, or draw, or do something delicate with.

– within a couple of days you might need to take a further statement as they began to recollect other details of the event.

With both Gary and Mason affected by adrenaline and cortisone they are not going to resolve this in a nice, mature way:

"Now look here Mason, I'm feeling a bit sore that you have said some things about my sister"

"Well actually Gary, I'm glad you raised that because I'm also feeling sore that my comment was misrepresented so badly. I actually feel that your sister has been very brave and I support her 100% and in fact any other gay person who is thinking about doing the same thing."

"Well, that's wonderful Mason – and many apologies, I clearly jumped to the wrong conclusion. I am sure that Rachel will be delighted and relieved."

"Not at all Gary. I can appreciate how you must have felt, and I have to admit I would have been angry too."

"Mason I'd like to apologise by buying you a donut in the canteen!"

"Splendid. That would be lovely."

Now we all know that is just not how that was going to play out. In that moment both those guys needed to walk in the opposite direction and calm down.

The presence of the whole crowd gathering around, gawping out of morbid curiosity and searching for gossip or scandal, phones out ready to film it going on, and of course someone starts a chant "Fight! Fight! Fight!" – that only sets one tone.

This is why, at this stage of the event, the only thing for both guys to do is to take a deep breath and walk in the opposite direction.

Stage 7 is now significantly important. This is where we get this much-used term 'beef' – which is to say 'a feud'. A feud is where two people, or perhaps two groups, actually stop caring about the issues and just get drawn into the personality conflict. Two people in a feud are *crazy* – they stop making any sense at all. One individual could actually do something nice for the other person, and the other person will react one of the following ways:

   a) "He's making fun of me. I'll show him."
   b) "I should think so – he owes me a lot more than that too"
   c) "I don't want that from him and I don't care, even if I do need it"

You see, all that matters is pride, anger, and the confrontation itself. It will *never* end – tit for tat – they go back and forward doing spiteful things to each other. Each time they do something spiteful to 'show' the other person, naturally the other person responds and does something spiteful back. They are literally just harming themselves. They cannot appreciate that every time they perpetuate the situation and keep it going, they're hurting themselves like morons. Back and forward.

It gets to a stage where neither of them can even remember how it all got started – *although both will claim that they didn't start it.* Ironically both will also refuse to acknowledge that they are invested in the feud at all *"No I've got no problem – he/she doesn't even mean that much to me"*. Ironically despite not wanting to show it, two feuding people are strongly invested in each other – even if that investment is completely negative. People can get quite obsessed with it, and it consumes them bitterly.

Feuds are really unhealthy and they need to be broken up – usually from an outside, impartial individual who can help both people to reflect on what they have done wrong. Not person A saying all the stuff that person B did wrong – but person A coming to terms with all the petty things that *they* (person A) did, all the small things, all the hurtful and disrespectful things. Person B has to do the same. Usually, both are as bad as each other because they have spent their time spiralling downward and matching each other blow for blow. Both people usually feel quite ashamed of themselves at this point when they recognise it.

Some of the worst feuds that I've encountered are between people who used to be friends, who know each other quite well, and at least at one time or another cared a lot about each other too.

When a fight has been broken up you do get situations where both parties remain angry, both parties feel bitter, and their immediate thoughts are about what is going to happen next. Both parties can be guarded and defensive – but they immediate start thinking about what they are going to do to 'get back' at the other person. As with everything we've described, it is massively unhealthy, it causes anxiety and fear on both sides (no matter how much posturing goes on and how much both sides deny it). In short it is very bad for the mental health of both people.

I've seen people join into this madness by taking sides, instead of mediating and being an honest and true friend. "Listen mate – what he did was wrong – but at the same time it wasn't a great idea to do _____, and I think we need to calm this situation down."

I've even seen *parents* wade in and take sides – looking each other up on social media or responding to things posted. It's even more ridiculous when fully grown adults get drawn in too – but it shows you the human capacity for this. A small spark can turn into a big fire.

In reality, someone has to be the mature person about this and has to seek the opportunity to mediate a settlement[18] – and that begins with someone reflecting on their behaviour and being big enough to offer an olive branch, say sorry for what *they* did wrong, and get round the table to discuss it sensibly.

---

[18] Mediation is where a third person helps both people to settle their differences calmly.

"Ok – I shouldn't have punched you when you looked away. I panicked. I was quite scared. I'm not going to lie. I just lashed out. I was full of adrenaline and I wasn't thinking straight. I'm not a violent person. I was scared. I'm really sorry that I did that."

This is the only way the other person is likely to start to offer something that is less defensive too:

"Look I was just really angry about what I heard you said about my sister – and I didn't even mean to get so aggressive. I wanted to talk to you, but it all got carried away, and I shouldn't have grabbed hold of you."

"I just want you to know that what I said got taken out of context. I think your sister is really brave and it's a shame that she has to feel nervous about coming out, but what I said that she was 'bad' I mean that in a respectful way. I was impressed by how strong she was being. People blew it up into something that it wasn't."

I've mediated a number of these conversations in quite extreme circumstances. It is a shame that sometimes it has to come to *such* an extreme before people can sit down and have the conversation that probably ought to have been had at stage 1 of this whole event – to clarify – that in fact, Mason never meant to offend Rachel in the first place.

What's going on with your hair Jez?

That's it! We've got hair related beef now Katie!!

Dealing with Conflict

Checklist:

- Be careful with your use of language. Even in humour things can be hurtful.
- Even language can be unreliable and mean different things to different people.
- When there is disagreement and the possibility of conflict, be ready to reflect on your own behaviour. Have you done something wrong?
- If you owe someone an apology, be ready to apologise.
- Use your empathy skills to see the situation from the other person's point of view – not just your own.
- Be careful who you trust and share your business with.
- Don't be part of the crowd that makes a difficult situation worse purely for entertainment value.
- Violence never solves anything.

Chapter 5:
The Importance of a Good Routine

The importance of a good routine

Routine develops excellence

Ok – we've had the drama chapter of 'dealing with conflict'. This is the business end of what makes champions! Finding a good routine! As any champion will tell you – it wasn't just a case of turning up on the day. As I have quoted elsewhere in this book already:

"Hard work beats talent when talent doesn't work hard."

This is absolutely true.

Good habits form and shape champions. The rigour of consistency – that is doing the same positive things over and over again – *that's what makes the difference.*

Bizarrely, I want to turn your attention to the fine art of Japanese sword making. It takes five years in an apprenticeship to become a Japanese sword maker. Even at the end of your five-year journey – the process of building your reputation only begins then. The swordsmiths create traditional weaponry which, of its time, was the finest technology in the world. The purity of the steel was unquestionably the best the world could offer in the high period of the Samurai – 12th century Japan. In truth the British industrial revolution, from about 1750 onwards (650 years later) was when the engineers of the UK really began to investigate and work with steel in any proper way. Nothing up until that period could compare to the steel that bladesmiths in Japan were working with to create their weapons.

A Japanese Samurai sword can take 18 months to make. One individual sword! Imagine trying to equip an army! The secret of the Japanese blade is in the way in which the sword maker reheats (to extreme temperatures) the metal of the blade again, and again. Heating it, melting it, beating it, quenching[19] it and starting all over again – folding the metal time and again upon itself to eliminate any impurities or weaknesses. It is an obsessional task that accepts nothing but the absolute best in the final product. The blade is scrutinised, reheated, folded and reworked until eventually what remains is absolutely pure and can be sharpened to an edge that is unlike any other.

---

[19] Cooling it down rapidly in water

It is, in fact, the routine, and the repetition of the skilled craftsperson that makes this sword possible. The repetition – despite the boredom of doing the same thing hundreds or even thousands of times. The repetition and the routine sharpens the blade, but as the blade is sharpened, so is the sword maker. This happens until it becomes subconscious[20] - the whole process of crafting the perfect sword becomes possible *without thinking*. It is carved into a part of the human brain where actions, repeated over and over again, can happen while the mind is already doing other things. Such a skilled person can do the most incredible tasks – while talking with someone else or offering their attention to something else at the same time.

You've seen jugglers who can hold a conversation while keeping five or six balls in the air at once. A different part of the brain makes this possible.

The sword maker and the sword produce each other – and each sword produced becomes a learning exercise. Each sword becomes sharper and closer to perfection. The sword maker improves every time.

The truth is that, once the routine is established – and if the routine is perfect – no talented amateur can hope to recreate or compete with the outcome. There is no beginners luck that can compare to what a seasoned professional creates. Likewise, there are no 'off days' – a dedicated professional, shaped by the routine of repetition

---

[20] Without thinking.

and dedication will never have to worry about a bad day at the office. Their eye might be so incredibly sharp that only they know the difference between a good day or a bad day – but the average person will only marvel at what seems to be utterly amazing.

Becoming successful at school doesn't require the obsessional quality of a Japanese steel worker. What this does underline though, is that shaping your routine, shaping your personal habits, becomes the process that ultimately will shape you and what the final version of you resembles.

First you create your habits – *then your habits create you.*

Developing sustainability through good routine

The consequence and the outcome of good routine is not only about developing excellence through repetition – it also becomes a vital tool for your mental health and your sustainability[21].

When people run marathons and exceptionally long distances they set off at an even pace, with a good rhythm to their stride. They know that they're going to have to keep that up for a long time. The world record for a marathon is two hours, one minute and nine seconds. It was set by Eliud Kipchoge who is the fastest man to ever run 26.2 miles. The average marathon time is four and a half hours – so he is more than twice as fast as the average person running.

---

[21] The ability to keep going with something for a long time.

Endurance combined with speed is a science in and of itself – a science that is built on repetition and routine.

Going off at your education as if you can get it all done in the next two weeks does you no good whatsoever. You *might* have the best results from two weeks of effort that you've ever seen, but equally, you might not. You might have two of the most chaotic and disorganised weeks of your life – and at the end, your results might be a bit better for sure, but equally, they might not be. The biggest question is – can you keep that up for the next five years? *Almost certainly not.*

A marathon is, in metric, 42,000 metres. Technically a man, the great Usain Bolt, has run 100 metres in 9.58 *seconds*. If Usain Bolt could run at that speed indefinitely, he would complete the marathon in one hour and seven minutes. If anything this makes the speed of Eliud Kipchoge even more insane – but clearly we know that a super-fast first 100m does not make the next 41,900m take care of themselves. As you stand with your hands on your knees, sucking in air, with your lungs burning, everyone else has another 41,900 metres to run past you.

[BTW – as an aside, and just for fun – why not challenge yourself to run 100m in 17.2 seconds. If you can run 100m at this speed, you can realise that Eliud Kipchoge had to run at that speed for 42,000 metres! Seriously – go and try it!]

What happens when you try as hard as you possibly can and throw everything you have into a short and very immediate cause, is that you burn out. Your body and your mind run out of resources, the exhaustion hits you very quickly, and you either have to rest, or you will eventually collapse.

Endurance is about building up your ability – like an athlete – to keep going for as long as possible under the stress and pressure of performance.

Every sport has an element of this, even sprinting. You look at the distance that you have to perform over and you must ensure that you can go that distance – it doesn't matter if it is 100m at high speed, 1500m, or a full marathon distance.

A Spanish runner, Ricardo Abad, set a world record for the highest number of marathons completed on a daily basis. Every day Abad completed another marathon. He kept this going for 607 days, finishing 607 marathons. This is very nearly twenty months of constant long-distance running.

You shouldn't be surprised if you decide to throw everything you have into a goal, that you suddenly shock your body by investing every minute that you have into that objective. Your body and your mind will begin to wonder, pretty quickly, what on earth is going on and, quite frankly, you're going to get sick of it. This is why a lot of people break diets that they set for themselves when they are going after immediate short term weight loss goals. They feel the need to cut out everything they enjoy eating and it doesn't take very long before they miss the way that things used to be.

Aiming for excellence and success if great – and sometimes watching the most amazing people do incredible thing is very inspiring. We want to be just like that. You have to realise that they began at a low level, and they built up to a steady routine that they could manage and sustain.

People who become excellent don't get up in the morning and think about what to do next. They get up in the morning and they look at their plan. Their plan is a structure around their time, and how they use their time, and they follow the plan and they stick to the structure – knowing that by a given date, they will have a specific outcomes to show for what they have done. They will have their achievement. Building excellent plans and structures is a specialist area of study that falls under the category of coaching. A great athlete will have a coach who takes responsibility for advising their athlete on what the plan should consist of, how much they should be doing, and when they should be taking rest. Every aspect of the athlete's life is on the plan – from sleep, to diet, to training schedule, to time off and rest. A plan takes care of every aspect and regulates the athlete. To some extent it takes the stress and anxiety and worry out of that process. You don't need to think about where to be and what to do – it's on the plan – *just follow the plan*.

If you went to the greatest Olympic athletes who are training at the moment – and you said that you wanted to tear up their plans and have them live on a day-to-day basis, eat from meal to meal, just go on instinct as to what they should be doing – they would be seriously worried about that. "Am I doing enough?" or "Am I doing too much?" or "What should I be doing now?".

We have already talked about the big question – what is your aim or goal for your education? Once you have that destination in mind, you can work back from there to prepare yourself and achieve that aim against a timescale.

My best advice is to tell you not to sprint off into the distance towards it. My best advice is to recommend that you develop a routine that carries you consistently in the right direction, and that you know you can keep up with, day to day and week to week. This makes it sustainable and balanced. It is what we call 'a routine'.

Daily activity is what drives yearly results

As a young police officer I entered a police organisation that was beginning to catch up with a thing that was known as 'performance culture'. Performance culture is about having individual officers and employees take accountability or responsibility for what that organisation delivers overall. What is their contribution?

Not long into my service my sergeant sat down with me and presented me with a sheet that showed me what my activity levels were as part of the response shift that I worked on (we were 'Band 2'). We were called 'omnicompetent officers' – that meant that we had to be able to do anything we were sent to. From a traffic incident, to arresting someone and investigating a crime, to dealing with a missing person report – anything. Some very different things in fact.

Omnicompetent means 'able to do everything'.

So I was shown how many crimes I had 'detected' (solved) in that month. How many incidents I had gone to. How many pieces of intelligence (information) I had submitted onto the police database. How many tickets I had written for vehicles on the road (fixed penalty notices or FPNs).

Very quickly in my head I looked at what I had to achieve per month and I could see that if I worked 20 days in a month (we worked on a ten day rota – six days on and four days off) what I would need to do every day to achieve a certain level of acceptable or successful performance.

I figured out a simple system that I called the 3,2,1 technique.

I needed to go to three incidents every day.

I needed to issue two tickets or submit two pieces of intelligence every day.

I needed to detect one crime (detecting or solving crimes was my favourite part of the job).

If I did this – every day that I went into work – by the end of an average month I would have attended sixty incidents, submitted forty tickets or pieces of intelligence, and I would detect twenty crimes. Over the course of a year that would really add up – 720 incidents, 480 tickets or intelligence items, and finally 240 crimes detected.

Now in reality that level of productivity – or output – was *not* realistic. Some days I would hit maybe two of the goals, some days all three. If I got sent to stand on a cordon and sign people in and out of a crime scene all day, I wouldn't hit any of them at all.

This didn't matter – because I knew that it was exceptional to detect 100 crimes per year and if I did, I would probably detect more crimes than anyone else on my team. Frankly – if I hit *half* of those goals my performance would be considered pretty outstanding. So that was factored into the plan.

The plan was simple. It was easy to remember. It was uncomplicated to implement. It took the stress out of what I needed to do, and what I was there to achieve. More than anything, it kept me focused every day, and I used it to compete with myself to drive my achievements forward.

I didn't arrive at this conclusion all by myself and I didn't get there by accident either. Before I was a police officer I was a salesman. I was selling mail-room equipment and quite frankly I found the products that I was selling to be very boring. If I told you about a franking machine – you've probably never heard of one before and you probably wouldn't be that interested in what it does. Actually, I'll tell you: a franking machine puts a digital payment stamp on a letter so that people don't have to put old fashioned stamps on envelops to send things through the mail. This might sound outdated now, but in 2001 there was a lot more stuff going through the mail. One of the things that was a problem for the industry was that as the internet took off, and email became more widespread, fewer people needed to send letters.

Put that to one side.

As a salesman I knew that I needed to be active to sell. I knew that I needed to have about three or four appointments with potential customers to sell a single machine to one of them.

I knew that to get a single appointment, I probably needed to phone about 10 different companies. This meant that if I made all my appointments on Monday, and I had Tuesday to Friday to do the appointments, I needed between 12 and 16 appointments per week. That also meant that I needed to phone about 160 people on the Monday to make those appointments. In an eight-hour day, I needed to call 20 people per hour…

Now – by working on my skills and getting better at my job I might change my ratios.

I might get to the place where I only need to call 8 people to make an appointment – *being better at making the phone calls would mean that I only needed to call 128 people instead of 160.*

If I could consistently sell a machine in every two appointments, suddenly my orders would increase substantially, *or I could work less and still get the same results.*

Finally in every deal that I signed I could think about my average order value – and if it was £8000 instead of £6000 that made a massive difference to me, because I was paid 10% in commission on every deal I signed. So instead of making £600, I'd make *£800 for myself. If I sold a machine every day, Tuesday to Friday, I would make £800 x 16 (big money).* If you focused on your activity and routine you could potentially be making £100,000 per year (or more).

Even now – making £800 per day in commission with a salary[22] underneath it – that is *outstanding* money. It was incredibly hard work – and while people say that selling is about 'the gift of the gab' or 'confidence' – it absolutely is not. It's about activity levels and it's about your routine and your sustainability.

---

[22] An additional annual income.

The truth is – whether you are in school, whether you are in policing, whether you are in sales – the ability to cultivate a positive routine and a structure around yourself that delivers the end goal, **that is a golden personal quality that will carry you to success no matter what it is that you want to do**. That is the hard work that beats talent.

Your routine

Ok so you might anticipate and hope that I'm going to write a golden routine for you here. That you can just read my book and adopt a suggested structure. Unfortunately, the trickiest bit of getting a perfect routine is tailoring that routine to suit the person (sorry!).

Even in exactly the same circumstances – two students who are preparing for A level maths (for example) – those two students will have different learning styles and approaches. They will have lifestyles and commitments at home. One might prefer to start early in the day, the other might be a night owl. One might prefer one topic in maths, and the other something else.

A good level of self-knowledge is vitally important.

If you know that you are not good in the morning and getting up first thing is really hard for you, sure you can get better at that with practise, but you're not playing to your strengths by scheduling[23] yourself in for a 6AM revision session!

---

[23] Planning in your diary.

One of the consistent things – no matter who you are – is that you only have twenty-four hours in a day. In that twenty-four hours you ought to be scheduling eight hours of sleep. You know what time you need to be at school for (don't be late!) and you know how long it takes to get to school. Additionally you need to plan enough time to get breakfast, wash and get dressed. If your washing and dressing habits take 45 minutes you need to build this in.

So let's start to work on this in an example:

3.15PM	School ends and you work on homework or study until...
7PM	Dinner
7.30PM	Your time to chill out
10.30PM	Go to bed, go to sleep (not Netflix in bed!)
6.30AM	Get up, wash, dress and eat a proper breakfast without rushing
8.00AM	Leave the house – it takes 30 minutes to get to school
8.30AM	School begins / Registration

Ok – so by starting with a fixed point, and the fixed point I have used is your registration time at school, we can work backwards and we can also work forwards from that.

What I have laid out is probably too simplistic for your needs – but you can adapt it.

Recognise that certain things are more fixed than others. For example *you do need adequate levels of sleep*. You absolutely must be in school on time.

On certain days you might play football or go to an after-school club. This means that not every day is the same, so perhaps you ought to develop a seven-day plan:

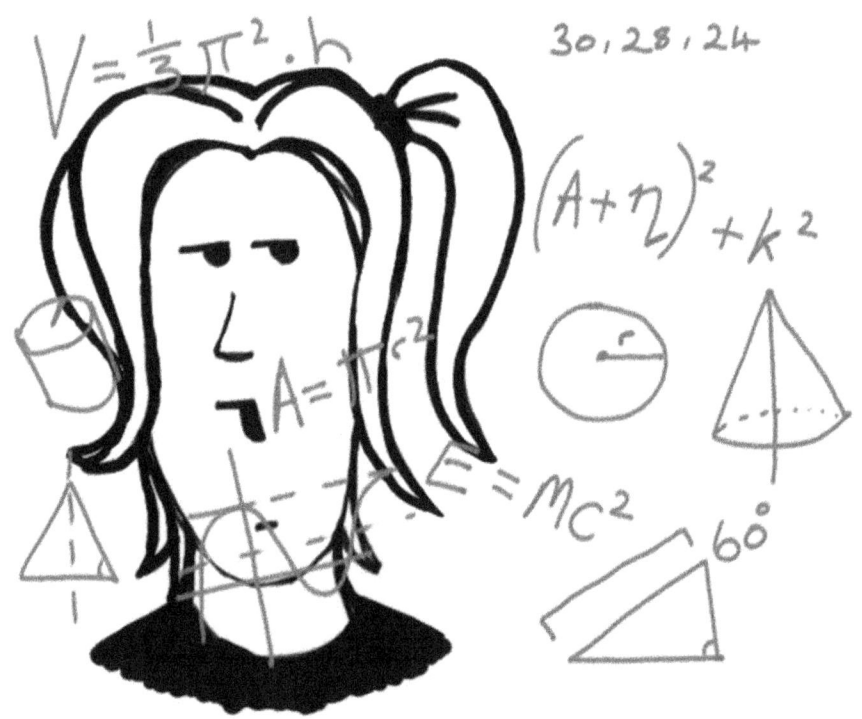

	Mon	Tues	Wed	Thurs	Fri	Sat	Sun
6.30AM	Get up – wash, dress and eat					Day off	
8AM	Leave for school						
8.30AM	Registration						
3.15PM	Home work & study until	Football Team until 5PM	Home work & study until	Home work & study until	Home work & study until		
5PM		Travel home, shower, then study/home work until					
5.30PM							
7PM			Evening Meal				
7.30PM	Your time	Your time	Your time	Your time	Your time	Day off	
10.30PM	Sleep				Late night	Late night	Sleep
11.30PM							

What we have developed is a raw example of what a schedule might look like. We've made sure to give you time every day to relax and unwind. You might find the idea of studying or doing homework until 7PM in the evening to be a difficult thing. I'd point out that, as you get used to it, it will become easier, and you'll benefit from staying on top of your homework. You never having to worry about it again! Your study routine will improve your performance in the classroom and as things get easier for you there, you'll start to appreciate the investment that you're making.

I am not saying that this schedule is the schedule that is right for you. It could be, it's likely to need adjustment for you, but it is intended to illustrate[24] how a positive routine could be built around you to help support your success.

Having a schedule of this nature is not designed to keep you locked down or tied up (something that puts a lot of people off) it's about helping you to make the very most of your time. Whether that is free time or work time. A lot of people use their time ineffectively because they're somewhere between work, rest and free time – maybe they're slumped on the couch watching something that they don't really care about. The time just drains away from them. They look up at the clock and realise that an hour and a half has been wasted... they think *"Oh there's no point starting now... I'll put it off until..."*. This is what we call 'procrastination'. Procrastination is when you actively look for reasons *not* to do something, *not* to get on with it – you know you have a

---

[24] Show you a picture or example.

task to do, but instead you can find five reasons to distract yourself. People do all manner of things to avoid the tasks that they don't want to do. Procrastination eats into your time – the old saying is:

"Procrastination is the thief of time."

It ends up stealing the time that you should have had to enjoy yourself. Having a schedule and a routine helps you to avoid procrastination and build the resilience and discipline to get on with the task – no matter what it might be. Doing this protects your free time, your personal time, that valuable time that you get to enjoy yourself. I'll be really frank – *we all deserve some time off and time to ourselves*, to do the things that we enjoy and that are fun – but we deserve it when we earn it. We invest in our success, we work hard when it is time to work and we reward ourselves when the work is done.

If you have a homework deadline on Monday, and it's Sunday night, and you haven't got it done – you have to make the choice. You either hurry, and get it done – often not very well, often feeling quite resentful of it and definitely not doing your best work (finding one hundred reasons why it's 'not fair'). Or you can consider what the potential punishment might be – you tell yourself "Maybe he/she [teacher] will forget to ask for it" you even tell yourself "What if they don't ask for it and I've spent all evening getting it done – I'll regret it then". You ask yourself "Should I take a chance? Maybe I can get away with it?". You actively tempt yourself not to bother. If you don't do it, in reality, you'll get sanctioned at school. A lunch time detention maybe, possibly an after school. It will undermine the relationship you have with that teacher. *It won't be good.* I think we've all been in that Sunday evening dilemma. It doesn't help that you're probably not looking forward to Monday morning very much.

Having your time structured through the week makes that scenario highly unlikely. You did yourself a favour – you got it done and out of the way. You even did a pretty job. You're even looking forward to handing it in to see how well you did. This is quite a different situation altogether – it's a much happier one.

A solid and reliable routine will make the very most of your talents and your abilities, it will sharpen your skills, it will keep you focused, it will protect you from procrastination and it will keep you out of trouble. You will be a much more successful person and you will enjoy your time at school a lot more too.

Hey Katie! When should we meet up?

Well I have lion taming on Tuesday — do you want to come to that?

Nope.

A good routine

checklist:

- Find a fixed point to plan your routine around;
- Be honest and reasonable about how long things take and don't cheat!
- There is no point planning to fail – if the plan you draw up doesn't give you enough time to cover your commitments you need to look at it again;
- Create a routine that delivers a positive outcome that you are happy with;
- Your school will already have given you a timetable of your lessons, use this as an example of how to plan forward and backwards in the day;
- Make your routine sustainable because you have to live with it over a long period before you will really start seeing the results;

Chapter 6:
Dealing with the chaos

'Chaos' is another word for complete disorder that is combined (put together) with a sense of confusion. In other words, you don't know what is happening or about to happen next. We've talked about having a strong routine that helps to frame your day-to-day activity and how the reassurance of that helps you to make the most of your time and what you can achieve. The chaos is what happens when it seems that, despite your best plans, and for no obvious reason, it all falls apart and it seems to turn into a mess.

There are so many sayings that encapsulate how planning is really important – but you have to remain able to confront the undoubted likelihood that the plan might fail in a particular moment.

Adventure starts where the plan ends.

You do need to have the personal resilience[25] to cope when your finely tuned plans don't work out quite the way that you thought that they would. This is a life skill – *a big life skill*.

This is not the time to give up and go home. This is the time when you win the respect of the people around you because you don't give up or give in. You sit down and you make what the police call a 'dynamic assessment': You consider what is most important right now, you identify your goals, and you do the very best you can to keep moving forwards.

---

[25] The ability to keep going.

You didn't plan for this building to catch fire – but now you're going to decide to save one thing and get the hell out of it.

Sometimes one of the best things about having a plan is that it gives you the courage to take something on that proves to be much more difficult that you possibly anticipated. It gets you to commit and once you are committed you test yourself and learn a lot.

When I left the police to set up my business I did not anticipate that a global pandemic was going to close all the schools that I would be working in, in roughly the next six months. My plan was to leave the police at the beginning of

September 2019, and I had agreements to work in four schools. In December the storm clouds of Corona Virus (Covid-19) were looming. *By the end of March 2020, the schools were closed.*

Not only was this *not* in my plan – there was absolutely no way to foresee it in September 2019. Nevertheless – I'm still here and everything somehow worked out fine.

In my local town a shop was being refurbished on the corner of a street near where I live. Previously it had been the premises of a local newspaper office. It had stood empty for some time. A local businessperson decided to setup a shop – right on the high street there – selling horse tack (equipment used to ride a horse). My town is massively into horses (I mean on an international basis) and so this would seem to be a reasonable plan. I am sure a lot of people buy a lot of horse tack around this area. The very week that they moved in and setup their window displays, the government declared an *absolute lockdown on retail* for anything of a non-essential nature. While certain shops clamoured to start selling some basic fundamentals to justify being allowed to stay open, it was too much of a stretch for this place to start selling nappies and cough medicine.

The timing was ridiculously cruel. It looked like the absolutely least likely event – a bolt of lightning – had struck this business. The new owner was now stuck paying rent and storage and the cost of employment and everything else – but without being allowed to open the doors to sell a single item. Heart-breaking.

No matter what your plan contains. No matter how thorough your schedule might be. No matter how you reassure yourself that you really have thought of everything,

I can promise you this, you cannot tell what is around the next corner, and you cannot blame yourself for that.

Sure, if you pay no thought to anything you will always be more likely to experience things going wrong. If you fail to prepare, you prepare to fail. So the saying goes.

If you do your best though – and you are diligent (that is, you are reasonably good at getting yourself ready in advance) you can expect people to be fair with you, and you give yourself the best likelihood of actually being able to cope with something going wrong. This being said, even if you don't know what is going to happen, you should keep yourself ready for *something* to let you down or become faulty or simply change at the last minute.

If everything does go to plan, that's a real treat, a bonus.

An old Latin phrase, that I don't expect you to learn, is "Si vis pacem, para bellum". It means

If you want peace, prepare for war

It recommends that you are free to hope for the best – but you are sensible if you prepare for the worst.

A more modern take on this saying is

I stay ready, so I don't have to get ready

This really is a state of mind, as much as anything else. It operates on so many different levels. Imagine: you and several friends are going out on a Friday night treat. You've decided to see a movie that has just come out and you're all excited about it. *What could possibly go wrong?*

Well – when you get to the cinema you find that the place is unexpectedly closed. In some recent cold weather, a pipe burst and flooded the place out. *No cinema tonight.* Now what are you going to do?

You already considered this and you've got two fall back options in your back pocket. You can either go and get a meal at a local restaurant for roughly the same price as your tickets and refreshments – that could be fun – or alternatively the number 5 bus will take you across town, it leaves in fifteen minutes, and there is another cinema over there…

What you don't do is call the whole thing off and go home and feel miserable. You don't sit on the corner in the cold weather and wish that you'd had a plan B.

Your friends are like "Wow – you're an absolute boss!" (and you are).

This is what we call 'contingency planning'. It's quite sophisticated, but it's about looking at any plan and thinking about where the weak spot in the plan is. What is the thing that is most likely to go wrong? What is the thing that you are expecting to go 'south'?

We all know how it works and if it all comes together, you're absolutely fine. In the back of your mind, you're thinking "Yeah but…" and that "Yeah but" that is nagging you is usually about the weakest part of your plan. It's the "Yeah but" moments that make chaos out of your plans. That bit falls through and all of a sudden the other pieces don't work anymore – you didn't really think through those consequences and if we're being honest, you simply hoped for the best.

That's why, when we go into an exam hall, **we have two pens**.

Now, you can spend all your time worrying about the details and making alternative arrangements ("If this happens, I'll do this, and if that happens… we go to this… BUT… if this and that happens, we'll do…") but you can't anticipate *everything* and you can drive yourself mad trying to. So my advice is to be reasonable, look at what you're doing, look at the day or the week ahead, think of the things that you need to reasonably be aware of and have a couple of options in your back pocket just in case. It's easy to convince yourself that everything is going to go wrong – and this means one of two things:

Either your plan is genuinely terrible (I guess it might be?) or you're being very hard on yourself.

Part of dealing with the chaos is about learning how to improvise, adapt and overcome the misfortune when it happens. You don't throw your goals in the bin simply because something bad happened and you didn't plan for it. Ok – in this situation something hasn't gone to plan, and you didn't have a contingency. This is where you develop two extremely valuable personal qualities. **Resilience and ingenuity.**

Ok, so resilience is about your ability to endure and keep going. You believe that if you can keep going you will get the job done. Nothing is going to stop you and you just keep moving towards your goal. Your car broke down? You call a taxi, an uber or you start walking. Your shovel broke? You find a way to dig with what is left of it. Whatever that situation is your natural sense of being stubborn and your determination combine – and they create this super quality – resilience. There is a sense of endurance – *that is the ability to just keep going* – and other people look at you with amazement. You might be studying and you decide that you could just put in another half an hour. At the end of that half hour, you put in another, just to be sure. You think of what the best of the best would do, and then you try to go that extra bit more. You're in the gym and you're supposed to do 12 reps on that machine? Just to make sure you push yourself to 14. Resilience isn't just about endurance though – it's not just about the ability to keep going. It's about a state of mind.

Some people set off to do ridiculous things that others see as 'impossible' – and they refuse to listen to that negativity. "No matter what, I am going to prove them all wrong". There are so many examples in history where 'perceived wisdom', that is what everyone agreed to be true, was left in tatters because one person had the strength of mind to push beyond that.

A really great example that I love is Sir Roger Bannister. Bannister believed that a human could run a mile in four minutes. *It was said to be impossible.* It had never been recorded and mankind had always fallen short of that achievement before.

In 1953 he came close – he ran a mile in four minutes and three seconds – which was amazing. He shattered the previous British record. For some it proved that it couldn't be done, man couldn't get that bit closer and that somehow, the four-minute limit was our physical ceiling.

Later the same year Bannister tried once again and this time he was only two seconds beyond that four-minute level.

Several other athletes were also trying – but they kept coming in at around two seconds over the four-minute barrier. Again, for some, this only served as proof that the four-minute mile would never be run by a human.

On the 6th May 1954, in Oxford, 3,000 people gathered to watch Roger Bannister make a further attempt. He ran it in a historic 3 minutes and 59.4 seconds. *The barrier was broken.* It was done. Almost immediately, as soon as that myth was lifted others broke the four-minute mile too. Today the record for running one mile is actually 3 minutes 43 seconds.

While resilience can be found in physical or mental behaviours, it is rare that physical resilience is found without mental resilience too. Very often resilience, which is a very much-admired personal quality, involves having to go through some measure of pain, or at the very least discomfort, and mentally you have the ability to absorb that feeling and carry on. This often makes the achievement at the end even more rewarding.

When people say that they are not willing to give up on their dream – it is their resilience that carries them through.

What about the second quality that we mentioned then? Ingenuity – sometimes called 'creativity'. Well, this is the ability to lose a part of your plan, sit down with what remains of it, with whatever resources you still have, and then shape another way to get the job done.

The next example that I've got for you is quite literally out of this world. It combined both resilience *and* creativity.

In the late 1960s and the early 1970s humankind was fascinated with space travel. The idea of orbiting the earth (flying around the earth in space) was a relatively new one. The history of space travel was incredibly new. Mankind had only walked on the moon for the first time in July 1969. This was the Apollo 11 mission where famously Neil Armstrong set foot on the surface of the moon saying:

"That's one small step for man, one giant leap for mankind"

A follow up mission, Apollo 12, also saw US astronauts walk on the moon. Apollo 13 was expected to be very similar and all the same plans were laid for further exploration of the surface of the moon.

Apollo 13 went badly wrong two days into the mission. A vital oxygen tank failed in the spacecraft, and it meant that the mission couldn't be completed. It also meant that the lives of the crew were in danger because the Co2 (Carbon Dioxide – poisonous gas) levels were rising and would reach lethal levels within an unacceptably short amount of time.

This one element of the plan could have proven fatal to the three US astronauts – Jim Lovell, Fred Haise and Jack Swigert.

Using the expertise that was available both onboard the craft, and in the ground control Space Centre, and considering absolutely everything that was readily available on the space module, they created an improvised Co2 filter to maintain the spacecraft in a controlled way and for such a period of time that allowed the astronauts to navigate a course back to Earth alive.

In a situation such as that – those three men were effectively trapped in a small metal box with very limited options and a steadily reducing volume of breathable air. For many that would have been a conclusive end to the mission and to the lives of the crew. The determination and creativity of everyone involved in the Apollo 13 mission meant that the men on board were able to come home unharmed.

While the situations surrounding you in school are unlikely to ever be life threatening – developing your ability to not overreact, to stay calm in the face of a difficult situation that is going wrong, and to respond intelligently with both the resilience and the ingenuity (creativity) to overcome what is happening – will give you a genuine advantage for the rest of your life.

Dealing with 'chaos' – in short – is about having a plan. It is also about having a back-up plan for the parts of that plan that you feel are most likely to go wrong. When the back-up plan isn't going to work – or the thing that goes wrong isn't what you made your contingency for (and you get surprised by something else) then you have to fall back on your *resilience and your ingenuity*.

Fundamentally though – at the foundation of everything – you never, ever, give up.

Remember this – if the whole situation becomes chaotic (full of chaos) – it is probably the same for everyone else too.

Think about the COVID-19 pandemic. When that pandemic reached the UK it had already swept westward from China, we saw it move through the Middle East, and it reached Europe, moving in through Italy.

Was it scary? I remember that it was *very scary*. Watching entire developed nations locking down. Not understanding the virus. Hearing about the damage that the virus did to people. The lives that had been lost and the loved ones that passed away.

There was no plan for this. There was no plan B either – at least not at a level of being in school. What if there is a fire?

Fires happen. You'll have fire drills every term. A pandemic was unprecedented – that is, we'd never faced *this* before.

'Unprecedented' means it never happened before.

Every single school was its own small community. Every school had its own leadership group and they had to toss the immediate priorities – the normal activities of running a school – out of the window. They had to go back to the drawing board and look at everything all over again and come up with new answers. It wasn't acceptable to just close the schools and do nothing. Schools do so much more than educate people. They feed people, they look after welfare issues, they provide friendship groups and support. They run social activities. A school is the beating heart of a community and more or less all of the children and young people growing up within a community will have that school as a thing that brings them and binds them together.

What I actually saw in schools was the very definition of resilience and ingenuity. Headteachers and Deputy-Headteachers displayed a huge amount of care and love for their communities and they never even considered giving up on the most vulnerable people that they needed to support. Knowing that absolutely everyone, pretty much on the planet, was facing the same challenge.

Further to that – *we all* had to display that attitude and follow that leadership and that example. We had to adapt our lives – we were locked down in our houses and we only went out for windows of exercise. We couldn't see our loved ones. We adapted and used new online tools to speak to family members and friends. None of us knew when it was going to end or get better. We dealt with that fear through a determination to make it through those days together, and whatever way we could, we found new ways to pass the time and to make those days more bearable. We knew that it was the same for the next family too.

It was chaotic, it was scary, and there was no real certainty – no plan. The government started briefing us every single day because of the crisis and how serious the whole situation was. Sadly – tragically – some of us didn't survive what we went through and so many of us lost people that we loved. Passing through chaos – going through such a difficult time – a time of national emergency, gives you something you can call on. When times get really tough, you can pause for a minute, think back to those lockdowns and having been through all of that you know "I've been through worse than this – so I know I can overcome this" (whatever the challenge might be). When times are very hard, that's what you do. You overcome the challenge, you outlast the challenge – and then you remember it. When you need that resilience and that courage, you think about it and draw strength from that experience.

There was so much that was tragic and quite terrible about the pandemic experience – but if you're reading this – we have that shared experience in common. Very soon a new generation of children and young people will have no knowledge of it and will not remember it or will not have been alive when it happened. It will be very difficult to help them to understand just what it was like at the time. As much as the chaos of the time was something nobody wants to have to go through ever again – and on so many levels you wish that you hadn't had to go through it – the resilience, the courage, the ingenuity that it gave to you is priceless and you will always have that to draw upon (and so will I).

Remember – nobody is born with these skills. You can't criticise yourself for having to learn these skills. They develop when you face adversity (hardship) – you watch the examples that other people give to you. You find your own methods of coping and being ok. You keep moving forward. You look to the people around you for support, and you support the people around you who need your help. It's easy to feel that you have to do it all on your own – but you don't. You need to trust the people that you care about, share your problems and your challenges, and you can work together to deal with what you are having to confront. No matter what it might be.

Katie! What happened to you?!

I got attacked by George at lion taming...

Who is George?! The lion?!

He's the lion tamer's parrot.

Dealing with the Chaos

Checklist

- Be ready to cope when things don't run to plan;
- Think about the things that are most likely to go wrong;
- Have a plan B!
- Don't give up, be stubborn and determined instead.
- Use creativity to find a way forward that works under the circumstances;
- Don't think that you have to solve all your problems on your own. Work with friends, loved ones and the people you trust to solve problems together;
- Remember – if the situation is chaotic for you, it is probably chaotic for the people around you – you're not alone!
- Never give up!

Chapter 7:
Have an outside interest

 I don't recommend lion taming. It's dangerous.

Here is a shocking fact for you: there are more honours students in China than there are students in Britain *in total*. That's at school leavers level. China's highest tier of academic achievement out numbers our student base – in totality.

How can this be possible?

Well the population of China is 1.4 billion people. The population of the UK is 67 million. This means that the Chinese population is slightly more than twenty times larger than the UK.

The availability of top tier intellect is always going to be hugely competitive and when you look at the international picture – and elite education is now very much an international picture – countries such as China (1.4 billion) and India (1.4 billion) are going to have a lot of very bright people – both in quality and in quantity.

If you apply to an elite university – for example Cambridge or Oxford – there are courses that are so over-subscribed that it can involve them choosing between twenty applicants so that one successful candidate can get the place.

I am not saying this to put you off.

Not many countries are better than the UK when it comes to education (the UK has a fine educational system when compared to so many countries – that is to your advantage) but you give yourself a much bigger advantage by presenting as a well-rounded candidate with strong abilities in other interests and areas too.

Students who leave school *not only* with the grades they need to get on the course that they want, or to apply for the recruitment scheme that they are aiming for – they reassure their application by demonstrating so much more.

The police, for example, has always been oversubscribed. Lots of people leave school wanting to be police officers. There are now also lots of mature entrants who join the police as a second career too. People who come out of other uniformed services such as the Army, Navy or the Royal Air Force. All these applicants bring so much more to the table than the grades they left school with.

Do not get me wrong.

If you want to join the police, or go to university, or get on a particular recruitment scheme or apprenticeship, you still need the entry grades. You absolutely do. It might surprise you that once you get over the line on those grades the difference between you getting the place that you want or not getting that place, is actually down to the extra things that you have done to demonstrate your personal qualities.

You are waving a flag saying "I'm not just good in school – I'm a rounded person, I have maturity, I have values".

Allow me to tell you a brief story about police recruitment.

I was a recruitment and selection officer when I was a sergeant. One day I got asked by Human Resources to go to HQ to interview candidates who wanted to become police officers. Interviewing eight people in a day doesn't sound

I want to give something back: my little brother!

like a lot – but asking the same set of questions *over and over again* all day long is tiring. It's a long day. It's an extra-long day if the candidates aren't impressing you.

Here's a quick tip to one side, by the way, if you want to join the police. We often used to ask a question that we didn't score, just to 'break the ice' and get people to open up and relax. Very often that question could be something like *"Why do you want to be a police officer?"*.

It's a more interesting question than it sounds because not only are you giving someone the opportunity to show their enthusiasm to you for the job (and it is a complicated and hard job to do). You also find out how realistic they are about what the job entails, and additionally, how honest they going to be in that interview. People used to think that the safe answer was "I want to give something back". *We used to hear that all the time.* I wish I had a penny for every time someone said it. I would even suggest that eight out of ten candidates wanted to 'give something back'.

"Do you recycle on a regular basis?"
"Sometimes"
"Do you volunteer for a charity?"
"No"
"Do you donate your clothes when you're finished with them?"
"No"
"Have you ever helped out at a food bank?"
"No"
"So you started to think that you wanted to give something back to society – and you thought that the first way, the most simple way of doing that, was to join the police?"
"Well..."

I could be cynical and suggest that eight out of ten candidates *didn't* want to give something back. Maybe couple did (I guess) – and maybe two could convince me that after serving for a couple of years as a volunteer in the Special Constabulary, and with the combined work they do at the church hall – yeah, this was the next big step for them, and they wanted to do more 'giving back'.

But being a police officer isn't about *'giving something back'*. Like schoolteachers, police officers are humans too, so as a consequence some of them are not doing the job because they want to 'give back'. I've even worked with one or two officers who I might even describe as being selfish – *that can be fine so long as they are professional, devoted to their job and they do it to the best of their abilities.* I'm not too worried about people 'giving back', my job was to identify some competent, honest, self-motivated and hardworking people.

Sometimes people would say something different like *"Well it looks like an exciting job. The idea of responding to emergencies, the police cars, the different things happening every day, the pressure, the fact that the public need you when things go wrong – it's exciting and I'm drawn to that"*. I always preferred that honesty. They might add *"The money isn't sensational – but it's decent, it's secure, and there's a good pension attached"*. Well now we're really talking in a truthful way. There is nothing wrong with being upfront about what is in it for *you*.

Anyway – *that's an aside* – on this day it was going really slowly. I had interviewed some of the worst candidates that I had *ever* encountered. It wasn't that I was in a particularly bad mood or anything – we were genuinely getting some terrible answers out there. In one case I had a gentleman who came in and his academic achievements were incredible (best I'd ever seen). He had a doctorate – that is to say he wasn't Mr Smith [fake name] he was Dr Smith – and his doctorate was in a field of technology that was well beyond my understanding. *What I really wanted Dr Smith to be able to do was put me at my ease with that and explain, in very ordinary language what it was that he was working on in his research.* If he had been able to do that, he would probably be a police officer today. I don't doubt that he was brilliantly intelligent, or that his work was complicated. Sadly, he couldn't communicate on a day-to-day level – the kind of day-to-day level that people need from a police officer who has to be able to talk to everyone.

Then in this whole desert of terrible applicants one young woman walked in. I won't name her – but let's call her Jane instead. Jane's written application was one of the weakest in the pile – handwriting wasn't very good, her grades coming out of school were below average, and there were a lot of spelling mistakes in there too *[Tip - get your application checked for spelling, punctuation and grammar]*.

When I spoke to Jane she was incredibly honest. She had not been great in school – had got into more trouble than she ought to. She had left with grades that weren't very good. She didn't have the best options, so she had to set about putting things right. She went looking for work and found an entry level place at a fast food restaurant. It wasn't cheerful work. She explained how she had to clean up after drunk people, mop floors, clean the toilets, deal with sick, people fighting each other from time to time. As a young woman working in a rowdy place, she was used to men putting their hands in unacceptable places (this is never ok guys). It was low paid work too. She decided that she was going to be the very best at it that she could be and threw herself into this situation with enthusiasm. That's why they promoted her to assistant manager in short space of time. *They could see that she cared.*

Now this positive attitude had my attention – but then she told me about her football. It didn't have to be football that she told me about, it could have been anything, *but she was passionate about it*. It was clear that she was a no-nonsense team player who like to step up and get stuck in on a weekend. She kept herself fit, she was her team captain, she but didn't play the star role, she made sure that the team was ticking. She tackled and she won the ball. She talked about the tactics of the game. She talked about her best game – which was against Arsenal ladies in a cup tie. I was absolutely drawn into this. I got a full picture of who she was, her values, I started to picture how she would fit into a shift. There are many, many times on a policing shift when you run out of officers and the incidents are mounting up and you're wondering how you're going to cover things, and you need someone like Jane who not only gets herself going, but gets people going around her. When you work on a team like that – some of the hardest shifts you have are the most memorable and the most rewarding.

Today, Jane does not have a doctorate. *She does have a job in the police though*.

I was determined that Jane was going to get the job. I was so impressed with her. I turned to the Human Resources officer that was conducting the interview alongside me – but I did not have to persuade her either.

We asked Jane to leave the room and we thanked her very much for her time (we would do this with everyone) and when we consulted each other it was very clear that we both felt exactly the same about this candidate. *I don't know what I can say that more clearly underlines how important the extra stuff you do outside of school actually is.*

More than making you a great candidate, having outside interests supports your mental health and your self-esteem.

You might have heard the phrase 'work/life balance'. Having an outside interest isn't just a cynical exercise in persuading people to give you a job or let you into their university. Just as the old 'I want to give something back' line is probably insincere – you shouldn't do things outside of school simply because they'll make you look good. Sure, if they make you look good and they reflect well on you – that's great, but it's not *why* you should be doing it.

When I said that 'Jane' was really impressive – what *really* impressed me was how much she obviously cared about what she was doing. We sometimes see modern politicians 'playing dress up' – that is to say they go to something, and they get dressed up for photographs (builders hat etc) and they smile and pretend to be invested in that cause so that people who vote can be fooled into thinking that they really care about that topic, that subject or that cause. You'll see politicians stand up in front of an international delegation on climate change and make promises to reduce carbon footprint one day, and then open a coal mine the next!

If you pursue an outside interest simply because it makes you look good, and because it is great 'window dressing' (that is the phrase used when people arrange themselves in the most attractive way for a given purpose, to sell themselves) you're not going to enjoy it. *It will become just another task on your list.*

If you can find something that you really care about that you can invest yourself in, that you love doing, your enthusiasm, care and love for that issue, will shine through. If you don't love it – *you'll be counting the minutes and the hours that you spend doing it*. People know the difference.

We've mentioned before – your mental health is incredibly important. It is critical to your success. You must support your mental health and you must be kind to yourself. This means that you have to find balance, you have to know when it is time to work hard and push forward, and when it is time to ease off, to rest, and to do things just for fun.

The benefit of having something in your life that you love doing is not about anyone else – it's about *you*. The time that you invest will be joyful. The range of different things you could consider is never ending. You might love sport, a range of different sports, cricket, tennis, football, basketball... keeping yourself active, fit and healthy is a really great way to invest in yourself. Speaking to one student that I have been helping and supporting in a particular school – he told me that his time on the football pitch is the only release that he really enjoys. *"I feel free. It's like everything makes sense there to me."*

You might want to start a micro-business. I know someone who loves making candles and has gradually structured a whole tiny little business around that enjoyment, making and selling candles by hand. It's not the revenue or the profit that motivates her. The sums involved are quite minor overall, but she is learning all the time while she does something that she enjoys tremendously, and as an activity, it pays for itself now that she has it running.

For many people the arts offer a way to escape the stresses of day-to-day life and the pressures of school, college or work. Fifteen minutes practising a musical instrument everyday will gradually accumulate and make you more than proficient. You could learn the guitar, the piano, or the clarinet. When I raise the issue of learning a music instrument, it is very often young people from less well-off backgrounds that roll their eyes and see learning a musical instrument as a fancy waste of time. The instruments seem expensive and inaccessible. It might feel like something that very middle-class young people do who are maybe a bit 'square'. In truth, if that was the case, there would be a whole generation without music because most of the great bands and musicians came out of a background that had no suggestion that music was an option for them. Kurt Cobain and Nirvana blew music away in the 1990s with a brand of music and fashion that was stripped down and very rough around the edges – but it was filled with feeling and with meaning. It became known as 'grunge'. People started shopping in charity shops to get that look – but for Kurt Cobain, Krist Novoselic and Dave Grohl – it was just a real expression of the fact that they came from dirt poor backgrounds where it was hard to make ends meet. For them, music became their form of expression, it became their outlet.

The accessibility of musical instruments is definitely easier if you're wealthy, don't get me wrong, most things are more accessible if you have a lot of money, but you don't have to be wealthy to play and to learn about music. If you go to your music department in school and you tell them *"Hey – I'd like to learn about..."* and you can be honest that you don't have a budget to get yourself started, I promise you – I have never met a music teacher that wasn't willing to go the extra mile to get a young person started. This is what they have dedicated their lives to do (which I think is a beautiful thing). By the way music is the number one export industry in the UK and it's a multi-billion-pound product.

Music isn't the only form of art that you might consider either. You could invest yourself in drawing – and again 15 minutes of drawing every day will make a remarkable difference to your ability. You might decide to write, poetry, or fictional prose (novels or short made-up stories). It might be that fiction isn't for you. Blogging and reviewing, or giving news commentary, or writing a chronical of the things that are happening around you – any of these things could become an incredible pastime.

"What would I write about?"

Imagining all that your generation has been through, the chronicles that are being recorded right now, charting the COVID-19 pandemic, and all the other extraordinary events surrounding us – these accounts will actually become invaluable historical documents and evidence of what we have lived through together. Writing for a local news site – or even creating one with friends – could be an amazing thing to widen your field of vision and to help you have a really worthwhile way of distracting yourself mentally from the stresses of the school environment.

All of these things offer you the chance to do something constructive and invaluable – that build you up as a more accomplished person, but give expression to the stresses of everyday life.

Perhaps more importantly you'll start to see a circular relationship between the outside interests in your life and the challenges that you face in school. The more you invest in the things you love and the more you develop an outside interest that really helps you to flourish, the more you start to clarify your aims and your goals for life and for your education. As you start to realise "It would be amazing to do this every day – I'd love to get paid for doing this" – it helps to shape your goals and your ambitions in life.

I often sit down with young people when they are feeling low – they are starting to get upset about the fact that their friends know what direction they want to go in and frankly, they just don't. The conversation usually goes "Well – what are you interested in? What do you do outside of school?".

They commonly reply *"Nothing"*.

Well – investing in yourself outside of school is really important to this. I then explore what they use their time doing – how on earth do they pass the time? The answers usually include either *"Going on my phone"* (social media) or *"Gaming"* (computer games).

Now, I'm not knocking the value of social media or computer games – and I enjoy both – but the problem is when you are simply a *consumer*. Everyone else is pumping out content and you sit and passively munch your way through it as if you're just eating chocolates at Christmas. You're giving hours to other people while you get nothing to show for it at all. You look up one day and realise that you've spent weeks and months of your life invested in something that has given you nothing in return. Moderation is always the key. It's not just that social media or gaming has not repaid you for the time you have invested, as much as the lack of opportunity that you've suffered from while you were doing that. It's what we call the 'opportunity cost' factor. You only have one bank of time – and how you choose to invest and spend your time can only happen *once*. There are no receipts and no refunds. If you spend five hours out of every day sitting on a social media channel consuming short thirty second videos you're going to limit your frame of concentration (you grow to want instant amusement), but you're stopping yourself from going out into the world to find something that is better than 'amusement'. You deny yourself a more meaningful sense of achievement and purpose.

Gaming is something that I honestly do enjoy and I grew up in the generation where video games were invented and every new generation of console broke new ground. I barely missed the release of a games console and I'm guilty of sinking serious time into particular games titles. I know what I'm talking about with this because I genuinely do not hate on games at all. *This being said* – I've learned to moderate as I've got older, as a student, as a professional, as a parent – I couldn't spend all day, or even all weekend – trying to 100% Red Dead Redemption 2 without expecting to see other things in my life suffer.

I mean – if you want to 100% RDR2 that is fine – but you don't have to do it in one sitting. Remember the chapter where we laid out a schedule and gave appropriate amounts of time to various responsibilities and interests?

I often encourage people who are locked into social media or video gaming ruts to consider how serious they are about this content. Do they want to become content developers? Would they like to become part of the production team? Would they like to learn about coding? Or video production?

Sometimes they say yes – and we start to work towards something from there. We can find an outside group or start to explore how we could put that together. It's a really positive step forward.

I have to say that most of the time they say *"No"* – and the reason for that is that they know that they're just using these distractions to fill time. They are distracting themselves from bigger questions or escaping from other pressures. In fairness, for some, it's an escape from the unavoidable: They are getting older and going through the daunting transition from childhood (where, for most, you have little or less to worry about) to adulthood (where personal responsibility and independence can be intimidating and even suffocating). This is a genuine issue. In other cases, when life is not particularly great for a child or young person, social media is a different type of escape or distraction.

Social media and video games can become a handy placeholder, you don't need to practise at anything, you don't need to be 'good' at it, there is no pressure. To quote an old phrase, you 'turn on, tune in and drop out' (a phrase created by a man named Timothy Leary in 1966). When the phrase was created originally it was more about young people switching on the radio or television – but the relevance is as true today (with digital social media) as it was then.

In a minority of situations media addiction is relevant – and at the end of this book I intend to offer some support links for people who are suffering with computer game or social media addiction. It's a very real thing. Some people get quite defensive about their consumption of such media – but ask yourself some fundamental questions:

Do you trade sleep for more time on social media/computer games?

Are you spending more time in social media/computer games than you spend going to school?

Do you miss meals to play video games or stay on social media?

Would you rather spend time in social media or gaming than spend time with friends and family?

Outside of school are most of your friends only known to you via social media/computer gaming circles?

If you compare the amount of time that you spend with your friends in person, versus the amount of time you spend with them virtually – which is the greater amount of time?

Being online and being up on what is happening on social media is fine – and you don't want to get left behind from things that are trending with your friends. However, sinking your whole life into media can be an empty and futile experience if it doesn't give you anything in return apart from moments of amusement, and it denies you the opportunity to explore the things that really could enrich your life.

 Jez! I've packed in lion taming!

Phew! That's a relief!

 So do you want to come to my motorcycle stunt performance instead?

Have an outside interest –

Checklist:

- Finding an outside interest that you love will help to guide your decisions on career and life purpose;
- It will also help you to develop strong and meaningful friendships;
- Balancing your life inside of school and outside of school will help you to create fantastic applications for colleges, apprenticeships, jobs and other opportunities;
- Having an outside interests helps to protect you from a over reliance on social media and computer games or boredom;
- Becoming good at something helps to boost your self-esteem and confidence, which is definitely good for your mental wellbeing.

Chapter 8:
Your Name, Your Brand.

The modern era is dominated by brands. While we live in a democracy where voters elect a government every five years, sometimes even government isn't as powerful as the largest and most popular brands. When the UK government refused to provide school meals to children through the COVID-19 lockdowns it wasn't the official opposition to the government that forced them to change their minds – it was the popularity of Manchester United footballer, Marcus Rashford and his publicity campaign.

I'd ask you to take a minute to think about your favourite brands. I wonder what will come to your mind? When I do this exercise in schools with students I get some popular choices. I often ask a student to choose their five favourite brands. Names like Nike, Apple and Louis Vuitton are very safe choices.

Just how powerful is a brand?

Let's consider Nike, for example and the 'Air Jordan' product specifically.

I've made references to Michael Jordan in this book already. I made reference to his meteoric rise through college and professional basketball. His desire to be the best – *the very best* – that ever played the game. He was relentless in his pursuit of perfection and on the back of it, his endorsement with Nike helped to build a brand that long outstripped his playing career and made him far more money than his playing career ever did.

Jordan, when speaking about his endorsements, clarified that if he wasn't scoring an outstanding number of points in a game, wasn't claiming rebounds and wasn't winning games – he wouldn't have been considered for an endorsement at all. He built *his* brand, with the help of the Nike marketing team, on the foundation of hard work and success on the basketball court.

Forbes magazine – an American business publication which specialises in tracking the values of businesses and individuals – suggests that the Jordan brand is worth about $10 billion (US dollars). This is a global mega-brand and on the back of this brand credibility Nike can charge around £200 for a pair of trainers that cost them £15 to make in the Far East. It has been suggested that Michael Jordan makes *$150 million* in royalties from Nike, *every year*. Just so you know, that's more than $400,000 every single day!

I'm not as interested in the cash as much as other aspects associated with the *power* of a brand though. In the case of Nike – and Air Jordan – there have been well published controversies. It hasn't all been smooth sailing.

In 1990, when Jordan was still playing for the Chicago Bulls, he was asked to support an anti-racism candidate for the US Senate. Democrat candidate Harvey Gantt was seeking to remove Republican Jesse Helms, a notorious racist, in Jordan's own home state of North Carolina. Jordan said that he didn't want to get involved because "Republicans buy sneakers too" – suggesting that he would sell fewer trainers and make less money if he took a stand. He has later said that he was joking, but despite this he didn't intervene publicly to support Harvey Gantt, and Jesse Helms was re-elected in a closely fought campaign. Triumphantly, Helms pronounced (with some measure of racist glee) *"Well, there is no joy in Mudville tonight"*. Instead, Michael Jordan insists that he quietly sent a financial contribution to the Harvey Gantt campaign – but (joking or not) he never did come out publicly against Helms in the election. Recently, former President Barak Obama, himself from Chicago and a huge Bulls fan, gently criticised Jordan by saying *"You would have wanted to see Michael push harder on that"*.

Another controversy connected to the Jordan brand has been the matter of limited-edition sales. Nike have been accused of under supplying the market to increase the prices they and others can charge. When desirable trainers are in short supply they sell more quickly and for higher prices to customers desperate to get them. The market has been so overheated that second hand trainers sold by fans (referred to as 'sneaker heads') have changed hands for four or five times the retail price. There has even been violence associated with the trainers – both in stores (where people have been known to fight over the shoes) and on the street (as people have been subjected to robberies to steal their Jordans). Michael Jordan and Nike have both been criticised, with claims that they could stop this by simply manufacturing more and by lowering the retail price to make them more available. Nike specifically seem wary of damaging the brand by making them more widely affordable and less exclusive.

Further issues exist around the shoes in that Nike could realistically afford to manufacture this product, sold at such a high price, pretty much anywhere in the world and still make a healthy profit. They choose to manufacture goods in Indonesia, Vietnam and in China, where people work for them in return for lower wages, with fewer employment rights and in worse conditions. As recently as 2019 reports from Nike garment factories suggested that the company was paying 'poverty wages' to workers, and there is a history of such factories having inhumane working conditions and unacceptable hours. Such allegations have been following Nike since the early 1990s. Human rights lobbies have pressured Nike for more than thirty years to use the massive wealth they have accumulated to eliminate child labour and people living in workhouse conditions. Despite this, the value and the influence of the Nike brand remains untouched and few young people seem aware or have chosen to reject the shoes on the grounds of human rights or ethical issues. *They still want Jordans.*

If there is a lesson to be learned here, it's that building a strong and successful brand can protect you from criticism and from the mistakes that you make. While I hope you would never deliberately choose to do any of the three things we have just briefly explored around Nike and Michael Jordan – it's clear that having a strong brand and reputation does help you to withstand the mistakes and human errors you are likely to make.

Brand building is an interesting phenomenon. Let's consider what we can learn and what this means for you.

You might think that brand building has nothing to do with you – that marketing a multi-billion-dollar image couldn't be further away from your reality. I'm going to tell you that I think you're wrong (and that you're every bit as important as a billion-dollar brand).

Every day we walk around, we do what we do, and we leave an impression on every single person that we meet, that we work with, that we spend time with. We build a reputation and people get to know us. This might be from the work that you are doing, it could be from the interests that you have outside school, it could be from spending time with you. The more they see of you the more they tend to have certain expectations. Such expectations can be positive, they can (of course) be negative. They might be correct; they might be incorrect. A brand – when it is built conscientiously (that is carefully and with determination) underlines and draws attention to the things that you do well. Additionally, a strong brand will have a *strategy* – something that copes with weaknesses and draws people away from them in the best way possible.

Right now – right at this very minute – your name is a brand. I guarantee it. It might be neglected[26] – it might not be something that you ever spent much time thinking about deliberately. *You could call this a 'brand' or you could call*

---

[26] Something you haven't consciously built or maintained.

this your 'reputation' – but it definitely exists. I could walk into the staff room at your school and say your name and the teachers will have their opinions.

I often invite students to go a step further from naming their favourite brands. I ask them to be really honest, and identify a brand that might be equivalent to their own reputation. For example – of the following clothing brands, where do you feel your brand is best illustrated?

- Louis Vuitton
- Reebok
- Levi
- George at Asda (Walmart)
- Dunlop

Perhaps the first thing to do is to put the brands in an order – from the strongest and most successful, to the weakest and least successful (in your opinion)? Then, having done that – think about the feelings that your name might generate in the staff room at school by comparison.

There are problems with this is – if you're low on confidence you might undervalue your reputation. If you're overconfident you might do the opposite. This being said, most people have a general idea and if you need to why not do this exercise with a trusted friend?

> I used to like Dunlop but I got tired of them!

Sometimes we all need to stop and reflect – and doing an exercise like this can help you to find out where you are right now, and also start to think about where you want to be in the fullness of time. An ideas board can be a great way to start building your brand and identifying your values. Start to gather the brands that you really admire and put them together on one page – what qualities do they share?

This can include the people you respect in the public eye – remember that anyone with a public image has a brand too. People – for example – talk about 'Brand Beckham' the combination of the work done by David Beckham and Victoria Beckham as a married couple. Their image was originally built on David being a world class footballer and the captain of the England football team. Victoria, of course was a pop star and a global chart selling performer in the 'Spice Girls' group. Since David retired from football, he has successfully become a brand ambassador for numerous commercial ventures (including lots of charities) and he has helped London to secure the Olympic Games. Victoria is now known for her contribution to the fashion industry, and she has successfully contributed as a designer at a couture[27] level. Both have been recognised with British Honours: David with an OBE[28] (services to football) and Victoria with an OBE of her own (services to fashion). Recently though David attracted criticism for accepting a reputed £10 million to take a prominent role in promoting the FIFA World Cup in Qatar – despite the questionable human rights record of that country. *Do you think that the choice he made damaged his reputation?* Do you think it was worth the £10 million he accepted? If you were in his position, would you take the money?

An important issue around branding is about associating your name with certain virtues and values – that is to say, when people hear your name, it inspires them to think about certain good qualities that you positively represent.

If you think about Cambridge University – you might have an image of refinery, tradition, and the highest standards of academic excellence. So if you meet someone, and they have just finished a masters degree you might say "Congratulations! Where did you study your masters?" if they reply – "University of Luton" how does that compare to "I studied at Cambridge"?

---

[27] Thought to be the height of fashion, generally associated with Paris.
[28] Officer of the Most Excellent Order of the British Empire.

The University of Luton, as a new university, are trying to establish their own reputation and credibility. They will work hard to compete for the same level of respect, and it is a huge challenge to compete with Cambridge, 40 miles away.

If we return to *your* brand image, we started to consider how we could get an idea of where it rests at the moment. It is very much about self-awareness and self-knowledge. Be honest with yourself – perhaps take a piece of paper and fold it down the middle. On one side write your better qualities. On the other side write down the things that you'd like to improve. For example, on the good side, you might right "Fun, spontaneous, full of energy, work hard, creative". On the other side you might be honest enough to admit "poor timekeeper – often late, sometimes unreliable, argumentative/opinionated".

Again – this is an exercise that you could complete with a very trusted friend (but you mustn't take offence if they're brave enough to tell you some honest things that you'd rather not hear!). You might write their qualities out, and they could write out yours.

Learning to seek feedback and learning to *accept* feedback, is an important part of building a successful brand. You can presume that everyone thinks you're great – but asking your teachers for feedback, or even asking your friends "Am I a good friend?" (for example) doesn't hurt from time to time. You have to be ready deal with the disappointment if the person tells you something you weren't aware of.

Let's be perfectly honest with ourselves, we are not perfect, and we are not going to build the perfect brand. In fact, the last thing you want is to project the image to others that you think you're perfect. *That really does cause annoyance!*

One thing that you must do when you have gathered feedback is decide how much it matters to you. This might be because of who gives you the feedback, or it might be what the feedback refers to. *"Phil is a nice guy, but he's a genuinely terrible singer and his piano playing is some of the worst I have ever heard"*.

If I was in the cabaret industry this might come as a crushing blow to me – thankfully I'm not (and when I say 'thankfully', you should be grateful that I'm not). Given that singing and piano playing are not that important to me (genuinely – as much as it would be a beautiful gift to have a singing voice and a music talent) I can happily agree with that feedback, and I can decide that I'm not about to enlist the support of a voice coach and a piano tutor to rectify those issues.

If I get the feedback that I do something badly that is important to me and that I care about deeply, well I might feel upset (that's natural) but I'm not going to take it out on anyone. What I'll probably do is get a second opinion – is this view *subjective* (i.e. just held by one person alone) or is it *objective* (generally agreed upon to a greater or lesser extent)? Is it something that I need to address?

If it proves that, *more or less*, the feedback was honest and I do actually have an issue to address, we have identified a point of development. A 'developmental issue'. This isn't the end of the world. In fact, it's an opportunity. We are all growing and changing, and we work hard to make ourselves better.

A former heavyweight boxing champion – sadly no longer alive – was the incredible 'Smokin' Joe Frazier. He fought in the 1970s.

Smokin' Joe was actually a bit small for a heavyweight, he weighed 205 lbs, versus his main lifelong rival the great Muhammed Ali, who was 215 lbs at the outset of his career and eventually fought above 220lbs. Joe was also shorter – recorded at around 5'11" (some suggest he wasn't that tall either). Ali was 6'2" by comparison.

A consequence of this was that Joe had shorter arms – a disadvantage when you're trying to reach out and hit someone with your gloved fist.

It's not that Joe could do a lot about these things and he didn't need anyone to tell him about these weaknesses either. For a great deal of Joe's career his strengths outweighed his weaknesses – and particularly in one department: His left hand was like a sledgehammer, and he delivered it in what some boxing trainers refer to as the textbook example of a left hook. If you were building a boxer and choosing attributes, and you gave that boxer a left hook like Joe Frazier, that fighter would immediately overcome most other limitations. Joe was tough too, he didn't mind getting hit, but he had great head movement, bobbing and weaving. He'd close in, possibly take a few shots on the way in, and he would deliver that left hook to the body or the head of his opponent. He would work away with it, coining the phrase that he 'got smokin', like an old-fashioned steam engine, gaining momentum as the fight wore on. Eventually, most opponents would fall to this and the longer the fight went on, the more likely it was going to happen.

The trouble for Joe was that he was nowhere near as dangerous on his right-hand side. A cornerman for Muhammed Ali, Dr Ferdie Pacheco (also now sadly gone) said *"He couldn't do anything with his right hand - Joe couldn't tie his shoelaces with his right hand"*.

So, when Ali and Frazier fought for the third time in Manila, in 1975, to settle their epic three fight rivalry, Ali evaluated Frazier (he actually said some very hurtful things about him). You could argue that, after two previous fights, nobody knew Frazier more intimately.

He thought that Frazier was tough, very dangerous on the left-hand side (Ali had already been knocked down once with that infamous left hook), but not smart or clever in the ring, and ineffective with his right hand.

Joe Frazier, however, worked on his weaknesses. He trained with his left hand tied to his body, forced to hit instead with his right. He learned to replicate his hook and his jab and his dangerous uppercuts, but with his right hand. In the early part of the fight Joe allowed Ali to think that everything was normal – the same old Joe Frazier, dangerous on the left, weak on the right, and not ring smart. When the moment arrived a few rounds into what has now been described as one of the most brutal fights in the history of boxing, Frazier saw Ali unprotected on the right-hand side. Lulled into a false sense of security and confidence, Ali was only worried about the left hand. Bang! Joe hit him with a painful right hand and doubled it up to his body and head again. Ali's eyes widened in surprise and he suddenly realised that the fight was very different now. He exclaimed to Frazier "You can't do that!" and he knew that the fight was going to be much more dangerous "There were two hands in this fight now" – a corner man said later.

This is one of the most obvious examples of someone not only learning and developing – but also using their reputation to provide themselves with a stunning advantage. Their self-knowledge helped them to grow and get stronger in every way. The existing image of 'Joe Frazier' helped them to deliver a surprise – and it was all the more unexpected because nobody thought that Joe had the intelligence to execute such a plan either.

Sometimes a brand image can be used to such an effect – but working on your brand and working on your image (and how people perceive you) is a great way to improve your knowledge of yourself, and the way in which you take advantage of your strengths and the perceptions of your weaknesses too.

Sun Tzu is the author of an ancient Chinese military textbook called 'The Art of War'.

'The Art of War' is a masterpiece in military strategy and tactics that has been applied to all manner of circumstances. It became more than a guide to the battlefield – it became philosophy. The fact that it was written roughly five hundred years before the birth of Jesus Christ, and survives today in millions of libraries around the world, is a testament to how powerful this work actually is.

His wisdom is conveyed in the following quote:

"If you know the enemy and know yourself, you need not fear the result of a hundred battles. If you know yourself but not the enemy, for every victory gained you will also suffer a defeat. If you know neither the enemy nor yourself, you will succumb[29] in every battle."

Brand strategy is very much about this concept. Are you knowledgeable about yourself and your weaknesses? Are you aware of what to do about your weaknesses? Do you know what you want to achieve? Do you know where you need to be strong? Are you aware of the challenge in front of you, and what you can do to overcome that challenge? Does your brand – the values that you uphold – support your efforts against that challenge?

If you thought that brand strategy was simply about impressing people – you might be wrong. Your brand strategy is about setting out your values and preparing to take on the challenge in front of you. As I write this, I ask

---

[29] Be defeated.

myself, *what good is my brand to me, if I want to be a world class cabaret entertainer?* Thankfully I do not.

Setting out a purpose for *your* brand, you automatically begin to take yourself more seriously and to value yourself. That is not to say that you cannot have a sense of humour about yourself or your weaknesses either. Afterall – I have no problem laughing about the fact that I cannot sing or play the piano. This being said – there absolutely should be things in your life that are not for laughing at. You are entitled to take yourself seriously and to choose what those things are.

If you are an aspiring sports person, no matter what your sport might be, you might want to look across a number of professionals and evaluate their qualities. *What can your learn from them?* What would you like to resemble? How can you copy the things that they did well?

Building a brand can be an act of creating something new, something that nobody has ever seen before, but additionally, it can be picking up where someone else stopped. In women's tennis we've been lucky enough to see some incredible matches played by some amazing, competitive athletes. Billie Jean King is known for what she did to professionalise the women's game and to demand equality in the prizes that were awarded. From Billie Jean King the game evolved and for many it was the great Martina Navratilova who carried, not only the evolution of the sport forward, but the quest for gender equality and respect too. Her professionalism, her power, her athleticism was the forerunner to the great Williams sisters – Venus and Serena, who each won Wimbledon championships and who each reigned as the best female tennis player (number 1) in the whole world. They broke records together as women, as athletes, and they broke the perception of the race barrier in elite tennis too.

You can set these great women alongside each other, they played in different generations, but they share qualities that everyone should admire and respect. They each overcame disadvantages and the perceptions and prejudices of other people. When a person has become a champion it looks as if they were always destined to be a champion. Sometimes they are spoken about as 'gifted' – as if someone gave it all to them. King, Navratilova, the Williams sister – they knew nothing about being given *anything*. They shared the same reputation for being incredibly hardworking and made themselves almost impossible to beat through their competitive spirit.

Your brand identity doesn't need to be 'original' or 'never seen before' – but it does need to be 'you' and you do need to believe in it 100%. Your brand needs to fit you, it needs to suit your outlook on the world, and you need to be comfortable with it. If you blew up into a massive success (and I'm sure that if you work with determination and commitment that you will) will you be happy that people who don't know you will identify you through these key principles and core values?

Being sincere and honest in what you project is important. In my humble opinion, the greatest icons are loved the most because they were true to their image, to their values and to their reputations. You only really feel let down by an icon that you love if you meet them, and you find out that they're really not like that at all. I've been lucky enough to meet a few of my heroes along the way – and I'm not about to drop names (because in all honesty those names might not mean anything to you) – but the experiences that really made me happy were the ones where I walked away feeling "They were really like I expected and I hoped they would be".

So be mindful of your brand and your reputation – inside and outside of school – it is not easy to uphold and stand by your principles and your values, but do it with sincerity, form the habits that repeatedly identify those qualities, and on the occasions when you feel that you didn't meet the high mark that you set for yourself, learn to be kind and forgive yourself for it too.

Katie! I'm rebranding myself!

What as? A magician?!

I was trying to look a bit posher and more sophisticated...

Your name, your brand

Checklist:

- Everyone has a brand. You might call it your reputation.
- Don't set out to be perfect – just set out to improve and get stronger.
- Be honest with yourself about your strengths and weaknesses. Perhaps talk with a trusted friend and do a strengths and weaknesses exercise with each other.
- Are you happy with your brand as it current is? *Do you need to change it and develop it?*
- Learn the difference between the feedback that you need to take seriously and the feedback that doesn't really matter.
- What do you want to achieve? Does your brand help you towards that goal?

Chapter 9:
How to deal with your mistakes

A great writer of the early 18th century, Alexander Pope wrote:

> **"To err is human, to forgive, divine"**

Pope was a spectacular writer of poetry and satire[30] – his collected works remain treasures of English literature. In this one line and just seven words, he said so much about what it is like to be 'a person'. No matter who you are, probably the one thing that you share with the next person – no matter who *they are* – is that you have both made mistakes in your life. There are things that you *regret*. There are things that you've done, sometimes making a simple mistake, sometimes even *deliberately* – and you look back and you think "I'm such an idiot" or "Why did I do that?" or "Why am I like this?". At some stage we have all got incredibly fed up with ourselves, annoyed with ourselves – we downright get to a situation where we might not even like ourselves any more...

Then we are confronted by an act of forgiveness. Forgiveness – described by Pope as 'divine'. I mean *genuine* forgiveness. When someone sees through what you did – the mistake, the act, the behaviour – and they see you. They realise your regret. They realise the remorse. They understand. They might reach back into something they did wrong and remembering how imperfect they are, no matter what the consequences of what happened might be, they

---

[30] Satire is writing that makes fun of people in power.

surprise you. They tell you – *and they mean it* – "It's ok – it's really ok".

Now accepting an apology – and an acknowledgement that you did something wrong – is important, of course it is. True forgiveness is divine – it feels like it breaks the boundaries of human logic because as people well... people can be quite unkind, even cruel sometimes. So many times, people practise the idea that *"You hurt me – I hope you get hurt for what you did"* (or worse). It seems unusual to see someone who has the strength of character to say *"I got hurt and I don't want anyone else to get hurt out of this situation any more – and that includes you"*. There are some rare and high-profile examples such as this one:

Stephen Lawrence was a British teenager who was murdered in London for being black. It was a horrific racially motivated attack which happened on the 22nd April 1993. He was just 18 years old. Stephen Lawrence was attacked by a gang of six racists and he was stabbed twice. He bled to death. His loss was a tragedy that sparked a huge outcry and resulted in a public inquiry. What became The Macpherson Inquiry (1997) criticised the police in the way in which they addressed and investigated the crime – both in the immediate hours after the event and later on. The report found that the Metropolitan Police (the police service that operates in London) was institutionally racist. The report went further than criticising the police and called for reforms in the Civil Service, local government organisations, the National Health Service, in schools and in the legal system too. Not only did Stephen Lawrence lose his life because of a racially motivated attack – the systems of the country let him down because of deeply embedded racism that compromised how the whole crime was investigated and handled. Despite all of this, quite incredibly, Stephen Lawrence's parents, Doreen and Neville Lawrence campaigned for changed while offering forgiveness and asking for calm. Doreen Lawrence is today a Baroness who was elevated to the House of Lords to support her work challenging racism in society. Neville Lawrence is now an honorary doctorate of Law, Education and Civil Law, he was awarded the OBE, and he is an advocate for marginalised and voiceless communities.

When you experience genuine forgiveness, I think you immediately want to make up for what you did (I know I do). You want to repair it in the best way that you can. Try and do something that makes good on the damage and demonstrates how sorry you are. You want to try to become a good person in their eyes – a better version of yourself – or at least a better version than the one you showed them previously.

You only get to this situation when you have the honesty and awareness to see that you made a mistake, that you did something wrong – and you're ready to confront that mistake.

Pretending not to have seen it, hoping that it will go away, maybe even pretending that the situation is ok or exactly what you wanted it to be, none of these responses actually get you the solution that you're looking for.

So how do we deal with our mistakes? What is the best way? If making mistakes is a natural part of the experience of being a human, being alive, it makes sense that we get well practised at dealing with it. Some of us make more mistakes than others – but I think it's likely that we're probably more or less in the same range.

Here's a few of the less positive responses that I've seen, and you can decide for yourself how successful they are and whether you think they're worth copying:

The cover up

Ok so we've seen this in politics particularly. Someone does something wrong. It might be a mistake that was made, it could be something worse, more deliberate – something morally unacceptable even. Whatever it is, the behaviour in itself is 'not ok'. The people or person responsible look at it from every angle. They can tell that this is wrong, even before everyone finds out. So, they fear that everyone is going to find out. What is the best thing to do? A carefully constructed lie, a false reason, perhaps an admirable motive[31] could take the sting out of this? Maybe the worst of it can be hidden from sight? This is where a cover up comes into play. By whatever means they try to hide their

---

[31] An attempt to find a 'good reason' to do a 'bad thing'.

wrongdoing, or if the wrongdoing itself can't be hidden, perhaps they'll hide the fact that it was *their* wrong-doing and pretend to have nothing to do with it. In a percentage of such cases, they might even get away with it. The nature of such things is that we really can't say what we haven't seen or what has been hidden successfully (otherwise the cover up didn't work) – so we can't really say how often people get away with using dishonesty to avoid their mistakes. What we do know is that, in plenty of cases, it doesn't work – the lies get all tangled up, and it comes to the surface looking even worse. Not only are you now left holding whatever you did wrong – *you look really dishonest too*. You took a risk, you thought you could get away with it, maybe in the past you successfully got out of trouble this way. This time you're in deep and nobody believes you because you got caught out telling a lie too.

The Blame Game

The situation is that something has gone wrong. You've got your hands on this and if you're being honest at least half of it is on you – it was your responsibility. Yes, there might be someone else involved and there are times when we make our mistakes collectively – two or more people running something together or doing something wrong together.

Now that the situation has come out and it has all gone wrong, the temptation is to blame the other person. You think that you can point the finger and look less guilty because, well, it was their fault, and you didn't really know that much about it?

"They led me down the wrong path!"

The trouble is that, in this situation, guess what the other person is doing? Do you think that they are going to sit there and let you push all the blame onto them? *Unlikely*. They are probably pointing the finger at you – saying exactly the same thing. "It wasn't even my idea" or "I got misled – I just went along with it".

Now the two of you are both guilty of wrongdoing and you both look guilty, and you both look like you're trying to wriggle out of it.

The 'Whatabout'

This is a really popular tactic that I've seen people use, and I'll be honest, it never really impresses anyone. The idea is simple. You look at what you did wrong, you think of an example (if you can) were someone did something just as bad, or maybe worse, and they managed to get away with it, or you thought that they weren't really punished for it. You then insert the phrase "Whatabout" and try to talk about that instead.

If you've wronged someone, maybe hurt them, insulted them, you look for a 'whatabout' that suggests that they did something to you first. "What about when they sent that message to me – that was just as bad…" (a little bit like victim blaming).

This is what we call 'evasive' – again, you're trying to wriggle out of the situation (and you know it). You're not taking responsibility, and one way or another, you just want to get off the hook. That's definitely what it looks like – even if the 'whatabout' seems quite genuine to you.

The Distraction (also known as 'the dead cat')

The distraction/dead cat tactic has really taken off in politics over the last few years. Someone does something wrong, something shocking and lots of people are talking about it.

To take attention away from that you think *"It would be great if something really huge happened now and everyone would be distracted by it"*.

Ideally someone else will do something, or some other event will happen – you get lucky – everyone looks over there and you get away from what happened. By the time the attention returns to your event, it has all died down, and people are no longer as bothered by what you did.

When that doesn't happen, a 'dead cat' might come in handy. A man named Lynton Crosby, a controversial political adviser, is strongly associated with creating this distraction tactic. Former Prime Minister, Boris Johnson described it in a piece he wrote for The Telegraph newspaper:

> *"There is one thing that is absolutely certain about throwing a dead cat on the dining room table – I don't mean that people will be outraged, alarmed,*

disgusted. That is true, but irrelevant. The key point, says my Australian friend [Crosby] is that everyone will shout 'Jeez, mate, there's a dead cat on the table!'. In other words, they will be talking about the dead cat – the thing you want them to talk about – and they will not be talking about the issue that has been causing you so much grief."

Doing something very different, but also controversial and attention seeking, you take attention away from one thing by doing or saying something else. Some people in the public eye have become so adept (so skilful) at doing this, they seem to go from one thing to the next in a chain of events and they happen so quickly that nobody can keep up. You hope that this blizzard of events will result in none of them actually coming to anything and you can walk away.

This is a fairly exhausting way to deal with a personal mistake though and it usually involves an unfortunate amount of dishonesty too.

The Personal Attack/Victim Blaming (also known as 'ad hominem[32]')

You've done something wrong, and someone is worse off for it. You might not have specifically tried to harm that person, but in the fall out they got harmed in some way by what you did.

---

[32] Latin for 'to the person'.

In this venture you try to make it *their fault*. "It was their fault anyway. It's not my fault that they chose to stand there – who would do something as silly as that? You can't blame me for that" (cyclist that ran into a pedestrian).

You might go a step further and attack them personally – try to win people over by suggesting *"Well they deserved it"* – you find a reason, any reason at all to win sympathy, or you might ridicule them and make fun of them. The effect that you're aiming for is 'So who cares if they got hurt?'.

This is very dark stuff – and you'll have seen people saying things like 'Women who get assaulted have to take responsibility for what they were wearing/where they were going/what time of night it was' – this kind of ridiculous statement belongs in this category. As does claiming provocation after someone has been assaulted or suggesting "They had it coming" or "They were asking for it".

All of this is quite shameful behaviour really.

Blackmail

Wow. Now we really are into the *dark stuff*. This sometimes happens when someone has made a mistake and it's the responsibility of someone else to shine a light on that error. The offender who made the original mistake or misdeed looks to highlight a different mistake or something embarrassing (relevant or not to the issue in hand) by the person investigating it (or perhaps they'll get a loyal friend will do this). *They suggest that if the first mistake (their mistake) is overlooked, they could also overlook the other matter.* The implication is that if the first matter or wrongdoing isn't overlooked, they will ensure that a negative consequence will happen in return.

This type of behaviour often encourages a culture where problems and issues get supressed, and the long-term consequences are that the environment becomes very unhappy and unpleasant pretty quickly. Blackmail is of course wrong, threatening people is very wrong. This is the absolute opposite of owning your mistakes and taking responsibility.

I could go on. There are lots of unethical and not very nice ways to deal with a mistake or a wrongdoing, these are usually bound together by negative motives and emotions such as fear (of being seen in a negative way, fear of consequences too), envy, vanity, or personal greed. They are also tied together – one way or another – by dishonesty. Keeping up with all this toxic behaviour is much harder than being frank and honest – even if being honest can at times prove to be painful initially.

One of the most high-profile cases of recent times involved a lady named Elizabeth Holmes. She is a complicated case in terms of her psychology and her personality – but the basis of her mistakes involved her belief that she could develop and deliver a machine that could diagnose countless illnesses and conditions from a single droplet of blood. She promised that a pinprick of blood from the finger could be analysed and within a reasonable waiting time, a medical report could be returned that would confirm whether the patient had any number of medical problems. In 2003 she assured people that her company, Theranos, had the technology to make this real.

The promise was, at best, a badly flawed one. She upheld all the lies for fifteen years. Over time it became very obvious that her hypothesis (her prediction) that this could be done was absolutely *not accurate*. She knew that her machine would not deliver against what she had described.

To cope, she lied to cover it up. She created a monster. The

I could be a billionaire. I just need a really good idea. And a billion pounds.

company that she founded consumed millions and eventually billions of dollars in investments from some of the most well-known businesspeople in the world. She fooled high profile politicians, celebrity talk show hosts, industry experts and even academics – before she was eventually exposed. The more she lied and covered up, the more excuses and cover-ups she needed. She attacked and threatened her critics in numerous ways. She silenced people who discovered the truth. She blamed and delayed and stalled on her deadlines. She even cheated on industry tests and demonstrations. *Her dishonesty overwhelmed her.* Her determination to be seen as a success become more significant than the truth that she was not successful at all. In 2013, her chief biochemist and scientist Ian Gibbons took his own life.

What is not entirely clear is how much Elizabeth Holmes convinced herself of her lies – but it is clear that her lies were very convincing.

In the end the mistakes that Elizabeth Holmes made – and the terrible coverup – resulted in her being sentenced to 11 years in a Federal US prison (with many commentators suggesting that she was lucky not to be sentenced to much more). Investors lost hundreds of millions of dollars - including the Walton family (who own Walmart) who lost $150 million, Rupert Murdoch (News International) who lost $125 million and the Devos Family (a business family in America) lost an estimated $100 million. *The damage was incredible.*

My point is not a complicated one – I don't advocate dishonesty as a way out of having made a mistake. Dishonesty only really adds insult to injury when something has gone wrong. When you are being dishonest, you're not only looking for a way out of trouble – you're also saying to the people that you're lying to *"I don't think you're clever enough to know the difference between the truth and this lie – I can fool you"*.

I think, at some stage, we've all been lied to. I think we all know how much it hurts when we discovered that someone has lied to us.

So the first stage of handling a mistake or having done something wrong, is to take a deep breath, and be honest about it. It's not easy, but it gets better from there (and if we're being honest, we all know that we've told lies – every single person has).

So, we start with honesty.

Now is the time to remind yourself "To err is human". You are a human, therefore, you make mistakes. You are not a machine. You are not a computer. For all the wonderful and miraculous and unique qualities that you have, that combine to make you the best version of yourself – you will have an off day too. Your judgement will be poor one day.

Start by being a friend to yourself. Be honest about your mistake, but the first step to that divine state of forgiveness, is being able to forgive yourself. In forgiving yourself – you also must remember that other people will make mistakes too, and surely when that happens you have to try to forgive them also.

'Beating yourself up' is another common response. It happens a lot. "How could I be so stupid? How could I forget to do that?" – ok, be angry with yourself for a little while. By all means. At some point, hopefully sooner rather than later, you have to calm down and move on.

Try to gain some *objectivity* about that. We've discussed objectivity before. Sometimes when we make mistakes, we start to trick ourselves into thinking that the whole world is going to fall down around us. "I forgot to do that, and now this will happen, and then that will happen, and I'll lose my job..." – it is easy to get carried away with such things.

Absolutely – sometimes a mistake can be very expensive. In the worst case scenarios the most expensive mistakes can be the most valuable of lessons. You will never forget them.

Most of the time, however, a mistake is just a mistake.

This is where talking to a trusted friend or advisor is a really good idea. They will help to bring you back down to earth with some realistic thoughts and observations. "I really don't think you'll lose your job over this".

Additionally – as the old saying goes:

A problem shared is a problem halved!

When something goes wrong and you're feeling a bit angry or panicked, you won't be thinking very clearly. Remember what we said before about adrenaline? *We don't think at our best when the adrenaline starts pumping and we go into high alert.* A friend, however (a good calm friend), can start to bring you back down to earth by reassuring you, by reminding you that you're still a good person, that the situation isn't as bad as you might think and by maybe even suggesting some good and constructive ideas about how to fix the mistake.

Getting things into context is important. You have to always keep in mind that no matter what the situation is, no matter how good or how bad, it will pass. When you're having a great time the speed of time seems to increase. When you're bored or things are painful or unhappy – the minutes creep by. The great playwright Shakespeare captured this in 'Romeo and Juliet'. When missing Juliet, Romeo exclaims:

Ay me! Sad hours seem long.

You have to remind yourself that time is the same – no matter what you are going through, and sixty seconds will pass at the same speed. A day passes at the same speed. A week will pass at the same speed. It doesn't matter if you are enjoying them or not. *We have no control over time.*

When my wife and I had children and they were babies people said to us "Enjoy this stage – it will go so quickly" – and I did enjoy that stage (I loved it) – but those years seemed to go by in the blink of an eye. I can barely believe it. Years gone by in the blink of an eye!

When you've made a mistake – believe this – you'll work through it, the time will pass (no matter how bad it might seem) and you will get the opportunity to recover and do better.

So be calm, confide in a friend or in friends that you trust, rely on the fact that you *will* get through it – and try to visualise or imagine how you are going to feel about his mistake a year from now. Will it even matter to you then? Will it simply be a lesson? Will you look back and laugh at yourself?

Now imagine something else.

A year from now – when that mistake is well behind you – if you had chosen to manage your mistake or your error or your misdeed by using one of those dishonest coping methods, *would you be proud of yourself*? Would it have been worth it? I think the only thing that would continue to make the situation sting and feel uncomfortable, would be looking back and seeing how you let yourself down in the aftermath[33] of what happened.

I am firmly of the belief that people don't prove themselves when everything is going well. *Everyone can look great when things are going their way.* Everyone can look cool when they're not under any pressure. It's when people are under pressure that people really prove themselves. In 17 years of policing, I saw a lot of people under pressure. I saw people under pressure when they had been arrested. I saw people under pressure who were cops – trying to cope with everything that was going on around them and the constant demands of their roles. I saw witnesses under pressure trying to remember what happened and do the right thing. I

---
[33] The period immediately after the wrongdoing.

saw people get it wrong and I saw people do amazing things and get it right.

I saw a father whose dog had savaged a postman (very badly), try to lay the risk of his own prosecution off on his wife and his daughter – rather than come into the police station and simply take responsibility for the fact that his guard dogs had inadequate safety measures around them. *That was a difficult thing to see, and an impossible thing to respect.* This man was very wealthy and seemed to have all the money in the world – but under that pressure he had very little character or courage to face up to what he did wrong. Looking back, I wonder if that father feels proud of how he behaved under the circumstances? I wonder if the relationships in his family will ever be the same?

His mistake was a terrible one and it had life changing consequences for the man who was attacked by the dog. The dog escaped his mansion, and the victim was attacked. It was a situation where I do not believe anyone did anything *deliberately* wrong to inflict such harm. It's what we call negligence – that is, the man had a responsibility to ensure that people were safe from his guard dogs – and he failed to take the appropriate steps to do that. In the aftermath of that horrific incident, he also failed to show the *honesty and the courage* that was needed to put his mistakes right and to be held accountable (that is to take responsibility). He has to live with how he let himself down and how focused he was on himself and minimising his liability or punishment – rather than being preoccupied with making a terrible situation right. It was, in fact, one of the worst things I ever saw when it came to how someone responded to a mistake that they had made.

In my experience it is very rare to see someone dealt with harshly, when they respond with honesty, with a genuine and sincere desire to put the situation right, and with a determination to do much better in future. Few people find that they are handled severely under the circumstances or that the situation comes back upon them in the worst way. Usually, in such circumstances, people admire the attitude and the honesty, and they apply what we call 'mitigation' to the outcome. Mitigation is where the seriousness and the severity of the situation is reduced. That is why when a defendant goes to criminal court in the UK, if they plead guilty at the earliest opportunity, they will always be given a 30% reduction on their sentence or their punishment for showing remorse and honesty.

The final piece of this chapter – *in learning to cope with your mistakes* **– is about apologising.**

Why is an apology important?

Well, it's not a magic spell that makes everything ok. You can't simply say the magic words "I'm sorry" and be transported out of the problem that you're in.

Additionally – "I'm sorry" is not *"I'm feeling sorry for myself and the situation that I'm in right now"*. That's no good. Nobody has any time for that. The worst versions of apologies include "I'm sorry (I got caught)" or the incredibly insulting "I am sorry that you're upset" (which is like blaming someone for their reaction to the situation).

An apology is important, because going back to our understanding of empathy and compassion, you are demonstrating that you can see things from someone else's point of view. You can now see how hurtful or harmful the situation is to them, and you're telling that person that you actually *do* regret what you did.

If you don't take the time to acknowledge these things – whether you do feel regretful or not – you definitely look like you don't care.

So, first thing, make sure that your apology is sincere. If it's fake, people can usually tell. Don't be fake. If you don't feel sorry, maybe you should take some time to sit and think the situation through a bit more. Spend a little more time considering it from another person's point of view. When you start to realise, and it begins to dawn on you, that this has had an adverse (negative) impact on someone else – maybe then is a good time to think about expressing how you feel about that.

Another important fact is that you ought to apologise to people you don't like, as well as to people that you do. If you owe an apology, the debt is the same – whether it's a person you do like or don't like.

If I choose to buy something the price doesn't fluctuate based on how much I like the people working in the shop.

The need to apologise doesn't go away because somehow, hurting people we *don't like* is 'ok'. It's not acceptable to say "They deserved it. I've never liked them anyway". The hardest apologies are the ones that we have to say to the people that we don't particularly like very much. It's very much easier to go back to a person that we love and admire and tell them how sorry we are for whatever it is that we've done wrong.

So having thought these things through – there are five stages to a proper apology. If you follow them, you will apologise in a more effective way and your apology will be more genuine and meaningful because of that.

1. Say that you're sorry (obviously).
2. Explain *what* you are sorry for – and why this is important from point of view of the person you are apologising to (i.e. as they would see it).
3. Offer to make the situation right in some way if you can, or ask if you can do something to make the situation right.
4. Express that you are going to take proper and realistic steps to prevent the mistake from happening again OR to improve on yourself so that it won't.
5. Ask them to accept the apology that you have offered (remember – nobody has to accept your apology).

In five simple points you will have made a thorough apology for what you have done wrong. Let me give you an example:

[imagine that I had broken the window of my neighbour, Mr Smith.]

Dear Mr Smith,

I am incredibly sorry that I broke your window. I want you to know that it was an accident and I didn't mean to do it. I don't want you to think that someone targeted you or did something to deliberately damage your home. I was chipping golf shots in my back garden, and I accidentally over hit the ball.

Please allow me to pay for the repair to your window. I want to make the situation right and I am sorry for the inconvenience that this must have caused you.

I can see that I shouldn't be playing golf in my back garden – it's not big enough and I'm not a good enough player to control my shots! I promise that I won't be doing that again!

I hope that you can accept this apology and that it won't damage our relationship as neighbours.

With kind regards,

 Jez I made a terrible mistake! I accidentally stole a million pounds worth of gold from the Bank of England...

YOU DID WHAT?!

 I accidentally defeated the CCTV and biometric entry system. I accidentally dug an escape tunnel...

How to Deal with your Mistakes

Checklist

- We all make mistakes and do things we are not proud of.
- Be honest with yourself and other people about what you've done. Getting caught up in a lie is just worse for everyone.
- Don't be tempted to covering it up or wriggling out of it. Be reasonable and responsible about it.
- Don't blow it out of proportion. Talk with a trusted friend. Don't beat yourself up – remember that you have to forgive yourself.
- Offer a proper effort to apologise and resolve the situation.
- If you want to be the type of person who can expect to be forgiven, you need to be the type of person who forgives other people when they make mistakes.

Chapter 10:
Drugs, Alcohol and Smoking

Drugs, smoking and alcohol are three of the most prominent and readily available mistakes that can be made in the period of your secondary school life.

I work with young people who are having issues with these three things quite frequently – and while drugs or smoking or alcohol might not be *the* problem in its entirety – they are a really reliable sign that a young person is in distress or in need of support.

There is a reason, generally speaking, why people turn to smoking, drugs or alcohol in their teenage years. While these things tend to become highly problematic, they usually begin with other problems.

I'm going to break this chapter into four pieces – three being fairly obvious – but the first thing that I want to address is 'addiction and dependency'. Then we'll look at alcohol, smoking (which includes vaping), and then finally, drugs after that.

Addiction and Dependency

If you have an addiction or a dependency problem, it means that you feel compelled to keep going back to the same thing time and time again. You feel that you cannot carry on without it. Your functional day tends to revolve around whatever it is that you cannot do without. You start to become obsessional and it preoccupies your thoughts.

Addiction is usually about a substance or a behaviour that the person in question cannot stop taking or doing. It's usually an unhealthy thing by the time it has got to that level. This can include things that appear to be healthy initially – until you take them to an extreme level. For example, you might even be addicted to fitness and gym use (which might sound really positive to begin with).

Playing sport tends to release dopamine into your system – something that is called a 'happy hormone'. It rewards you for doing well and makes you feel good. When that dopamine hit comes, you get a sense of enjoyment or pleasure from what you did. So you might have scored a wonderful goal playing football – and over time you get to like that feeling so much that you then end up addicted to

Video game and social media addictions are real things too.

playing football and scoring goals. Every time you score you feel brilliant, and you just want to play more and more football.

In the case of running long distances there have been people who have got that dopamine hit from going out for long runs – but end up running harder and further all the time, until they are doing such long-distance sessions that the pressure and the impact on their knees and joints ends up causing serious injuries. Most things, without moderation, if performed to an excessive level, can become harmful.

Ever eaten so much chocolate cake that you ended up making yourself feel sick? So much that you never want to see a cake again? For some people that point doesn't come. Eating a slice of delicious cake is a pleasure. Eating cake after cake will eventually lead to morbid obesity (a fatal level of weight gain that puts excessive pressure on your vital organs and eventually kills you).

There are lots of things that are commonly associated with addiction, however. Some things are more addictive or likely to result in dependency – we know that alcohol, smoking and drugs all have such risks attached to them.

Dependency happens when you get to such a stage that if you don't have at least a certain amount of that substance or activity, your body starts to go into a painful process we call 'withdrawal' and you feel unwell. You can't function properly. Withdrawal doesn't last forever, but it can last for a month in certain circumstances. It can be incredibly painful and might plunge you into a low mood or a state of depression as your body and brain readjust to life without whatever it was that you were addicted to. For many people withdrawal is so severely uncomfortable or painful that they go back to their addiction instead. Withdrawal has many symptoms, and in extreme circumstances (such as withdrawing from cocaine abuse) it can include such things as vomiting, stomach pains, being unable to sleep, having a fever, aches and pains. A person's mental health often suffers when they go through withdrawal. A person might even feel suicidal for a period of time. When a person goes 'cold turkey' (they suddenly stop doing or using whatever it was that they were addicted to) they go downhill quickly, they are plunged into the withdrawal and this can be very dangerous. In certain circumstances it can even be fatal. So withdrawal has to be managed carefully and in consultation with a doctor.

When a person recognises that they have an addiction and dependency issue the most sensible thing for them to do is to seek medical advice. Addiction and dependency are genuine medical issues. A qualified doctor can monitor the process of withdrawal gradually to make it more comfortable and to make it safer and more successful.

Addiction and dependency are illnesses that need to be managed. If you feel that you are suffering from an addiction, you should ask for help – no matter what the problem behaviour or substance is. A lot of people have felt a sense of shame when they had to admit to an addiction – their addiction might have brought them into behaviours that they that they regretted enormously. No matter what the issue is, you can be free of the problem, but you need support and it might be something that you need to manage quite carefully for the rest of your life.

Some substances *are* more addictive than others – that is to say there is a much higher likelihood of becoming addicted, and the process of becoming addicted might happen much more quickly than when compared to something else that is *less* addictive.

There is a lot of research being conducted into refined sugar (for example) – which is used in so many of the things that we eat. Sugar addiction is 'a thing'. Refined sugar has been tested on rats in laboratories and findings have suggested that it can be as addictive as heroin or cocaine. Some of the things that are highly addictive can be quite surprising and many are part of our everyday life. This includes caffeine – which is probably my personal addiction because I drink several cups of coffee every day. It is not simply whether a substance is addictive or not that causes it to be listed as illegal. There are many substances that are legal to consume that can lead to addiction.

It is important to understand that addiction and dependency is not just something that happens to 'someone else'. Addiction can happen to anyone and there are lots of circumstances where it is absolutely not their fault that it happened either. I would encourage you not to be judgemental of people who have an addiction that they are managing or coming to terms with. It is not a character flaw. Remember that addiction is a life changing illness.

I will list some resources to help you to identify whether you feel you have a problem with addiction and dependency at the end of this book. I will also list some resources that help you to find expert knowledge on what to do if addiction and dependency is a problem for you or a person you love.

Alcohol

Let's begin by looking at alcohol. Alcohol is something that can be addictive and has killed many hundreds of thousands people in the UK alone. The Office of National Statistics (ONS) suggests that 9,641 people died of alcohol specific causes in the UK in 2021. This is a worrying number indeed and a substantial increase on 2020 when 8,974 people died in the same classified circumstances.

So alcohol can be a lethal substance, it can lead to addiction, and the effect of alcohol in the UK is getting worse. Furthermore, alcohol, even when it is not lethal, is linked to crime and antisocial behaviour. The police and ambulance services have to spend billions of pounds per year responding to fights, injuries and accidents caused by people drinking excessively.

You may well ask – why on earth is alcohol legal then?

We know that historically prohibition movements (which outlawed the consumption of alcohol) have not worked. One of the largest examples was the period of national prohibition in the United States of America, 1920 until 1933.

This was a 13-year period that allowed us to understand the effects of making alcoholic drinks illegal – and generally speaking it was found that the drinks continued to be manufactured and consumed, however the safety standards around them fell, while profits recorded through organised criminality soared. Given that such an extended period was devoted to trying to take alcohol out of circulation in a large and developed nation – but failed – we tend to believe that regulating the supply of alcohol is a far safer option for everyone.

In the United Kingdom it is illegal to serve alcohol to a person under the age of 18. While the law has remained the same on this for a long time – more recently, licensed premises have been encouraged not to sell alcohol to anyone who looks under 21, if they don't have evidence that they are over 18.

We have to take alcohol seriously.

In moderation alcohol is absolutely fine – and a lot of young people are introduced to it by their parents. Perhaps they'll drink some of their Dad's beer to find out if they like the taste, or they might have a glass of wine with a family dinner as they get a bit older. In moderation there is safety.

Of course, nobody should ever drink and drive – and while there is a drink/drive limit in the UK (an amount that you can drink and be considered still fit to drive) – drinking and driving is hugely frowned upon and it is far better not to drink at all if you're going to get behind the wheel of a car or ride a moped or motorcycle.

Most people do get to a certain age where they drink to excess and they do it deliberately. I absolutely admit that I was one of those people. It's almost a 'rite of passage' – something that you do when you get to a certain age. For some it's when they *look* old enough to get served in a pub. For others it's when they hit 18. For me, when I went away to University it was something that everyone was doing and it wasn't even something that I felt that I needed to do to fit in – I just wanted to do it too! It seemed exciting and there was a lot going on, the parties were great fun, my friends were doing it... I more than happily joined in. I wasn't subjected to peer pressure even if many commentators have asked questions about whether the UK specifically has a 'drinking culture'.

Thankfully I didn't get myself into any trouble. I never drove a car after drinking, I didn't develop addiction problems, and when I was drunk I didn't do anything stupid that might have got me arrested, or might have hurt me. I'm not an aggressive person when I'm drunk. Alcohol does change our behaviour though; it extends our moods, and it loosens our inhibitions (our self control) – so behaviour when drunk can be a problem!

The state of being drunk – or 'intoxicated' – is a strange one. Alcohol interacts with your brain function in a way that clouds your judgement, it makes you disoriented, it limits your recall of information, it can make it difficult to perform even the simple tasks like tying your shoelace – or if you're really drunk – walking in a straight line. The more you drink the harder it is to function.

You might think that you can hide the effect and that people won't notice if you're drunk – but generally everyone will know straight away.

Alcohol can give you false confidence. It can make you say what is on your mind without being concerned about how that will impact on other people. It can makes you more 'extroverted' – that is far less shy and worried about yourself and what people think of you. *An old saying is that two types of people tell the absolute truth – children and drunk people!*

As a consequence, you can seriously embarrass yourself when you're drunk. More than that, you can choose to do things when you are drunk that you would definitely not do if you were sober. It can also impair your recollection of the facts and the circumstances – and you might wake up not remembering exactly what it was that you did. "How did that traffic cone get into my bedroom?"

For a lot of young people, drinking happens in public places and after dark. These two combined factors add an extra layer of risk to what they are doing. You might start an evening in the park with your friends and someone is passing around a bottle of something – you might not be aware of how strong the alcohol is in that drink. You drink too much of it and begin to feel much more confident and happy. You lose your way – you realise that you are no longer with your friends but you're not quite sure how *that* happened. You might become isolated and suddenly now – as a teenager, after dark, out alone, you are exceptionally vulnerable. *Particularly if you are alone with someone you don't know or someone who has isolated you deliberately.*

When alcohol is mixed with other things it gets more risky.

Never mix alcohol and paracetamol – the consequences can be very dangerous.

You don't know how it will interact with different substances or drugs – did you know that the common painkiller paracetamol and alcohol shouldn't be mixed for example?

Many music videos show people smoking cannabis (weed) and drinking alcohol and again this is a really bad combination because each of these substances exaggerates the effect that the other one has. Alcohol will make the cannabis feel stronger, and the weed will do the same to the alcohol too.

Alcohol can make people feel more sexually permissive (i.e. more likely to say yes to sexual behaviour) – but the combination of alcohol and sex is rarely a good one. **Sex is something that should always be completely consensual** – but alcohol is something that can undermine a person's ability to give **true** (genuine) consent. Who wants to sleep with someone thinking "They only had sex with me because they were drunk"?

As a young person you should know that the age of consent to sex is 16, you should be over 16 and your partner should be over 16 too. Additionally, and for good reasons, I'd recommend that you ought to be sober (both of you) and finally you should be practising contraception. There are many cases where unplanned pregnancies happen as a consequence of poor judgement and sex that has taken place when people are drunk.

There is a high likelihood that you will be offered alcohol during your teenage years. While you might think that you don't want to drink with adults around – actually having a trusted adult on hand is a pretty good idea as you get used to what alcohol makes you feel like. You might drink at a family wedding, but having your parents and family there might just help to keep things a bit more moderate. That is not a bad thing at all.

You are the only one that can weigh up whether it is a good idea for you to accept a drink in the circumstances that you find yourself in. Remember – you can always turn a drink down by saying something like "Nah, I've not been feeling very well" or simply "No thanks – I don't feel like it".

It is really not very cool at all to try to pressure anyone into drinking – and if you're with someone or a group of people who are trying to do that to you, it's a bit of a red flag and you might want to reconsider your friendship group.

If someone does buy you a drink – and you don't see the drink being poured or the bottle being opened – be mindful of drink spiking (which has also been an increasing problem). Drink spiking is when someone puts an unknown substance in your drink likely to have a strong impact on your ability to think clearly and say no or give true consent to (in most cases) sexual activity. If you think there is something wrong with your drink, if you have left your drink alone for any period of time, or if you simply don't trust the person who has handed you the drink – just get rid of it. In the worst-case scenario just pretend to spill it or quietly pour it away.

A massive problem with alcohol, if you do find yourself addicted to it, is that it is more or less everywhere. As soon as you open your eyes to it, you realise that society is almost framed by the use of alcohol. When a baby is born? We 'wet the baby's head' and drink. Almost every significant holiday in the calendar has drink attached to it. Most corner shops are 'off licences' (shops that sell alcohol to be consumed off premises). Pretty much every restaurant is also a bar, or has a bar. While you wait for your table? Sit at the bar. A person plucks up the courage to ask another out "Would you like to go for a drink sometime?". Whereas smoking, vaping and drug taking are all questioned, frowned upon or warned against – there is a fairly solid expectation that when you get to a certain age, you'll start drinking. To such an extent that people can even ask "What's your drink?" or "What do you drink?". If you're an adult and you respond "I don't really" or you offer a soft drink "I'll have a lime and soda water please" there is a presumption that either you're the driver tonight or "Does he/she have a drink problem?".

Look – I'm not anti-drink. In moderation, I have enjoyed drink and I do enjoy drink – but I also recognise the problems attached to drink. I see the issues around drinking cultures and how we somehow value those who can drink a lot ('hold their drink') and I have seen the issues associated with alcohol poisoning, addiction and dependency. What I'm saying is that, the temptation towards drink as you become a teenager, and as your teenage years become more advanced, is definitely strong. *There is pressure to drink.* When you hit 18 there is almost an expectation that one of the first things you will immediately go out and do is get very drunk to 'celebrate' your adulthood in a blur of incoherence that you can barely remember. You'll 'buy your first drink'. The recklessness that we encourage with drink is pretty irresponsible at times and we normalise this in the UK in a way that some other national cultures don't. So when it comes to drink – look at it objectively, take your time, and don't feel like you have to keep up with the expectations or pressures.

Smoking

So let's talk about smoking – and when it comes to that, what about vaping too?

Smoking first. We all ought to know by now that smoking is a hideously expensive, it is deadly and it is a highly addictive pastime. There is literally no upside, no benefit and nothing good to be said about it.

It is ruinously expensive. A twenty pack of cigarettes in a UK supermarket will cost about £15. In 2017 an EU survey suggested that 91% of smokers were smoking 10 cigarettes per day – 53% said more than 20[34]. In such circumstances those smokers are spending between £7.50 per day and £15. Per day! An 'extreme' group of 8% are spending more than £15 per day. Remember if the use increases by 10 cigarettes per day, it costs an additional £7.50 per day. So a 30-cigarette per-day habit – *which is nearly a cigarette every half hour of the average waking day* – is costing £22.50 (per day).

Those 10 daily cigarettes cost around £2700 per year, 20 cost you £5,400 per year, and a 30 per day habit costs you – wow – an astonishing **£8200** per year.

The average salary in the UK at the time of writing – in the middle of a cost-of -living crisis – for 18 – 21 year olds is £19,248 (according to the government). *Now take £8,000 off that for smoking heavily...*

---

[34] Statista, May 2017 – 7,168 respondents aged 15 years and over.

I do not have to talk you through what you could buy with that money instead – particularly if you saved it (or some of it) from year to year.

If you're already smoking, you might read this and say: "I roll my own and it's cheaper". Well ASH Scotland [35] have published data to suggest that rolling your own cigarettes is roughly *half* as expensive. They believe that in Scotland the average smoker consumes 12 cigarettes per day (men slightly more, women slightly less) and the amount that people are smoking is declining.

12 cigarettes at half the cost that we already calculated still comes out at a hefty £1600 (ish) per year – or you having to find £130-£140 per month. *You can definitely buy a very reasonable car for that.*

So let's get beyond the financials. Apart from it emptying your bank account on the regular, what does smoking do for you?

Well – it pretty much increases your likelihood of developing every illness you can imagine, and mostly the really horrendous and nasty ones.

We can start with cancer – because everyone knows that smoking causes cancer. Lung diseases are next – apart from cancer, you have bronchitis and emphysema too. Both of those are caused when the lungs are damaged – they result in painful symptoms, coughing, shortness of breath and of

---

[35] Action on Smoking & Health – ashscotland.org.uk

course that nasty yellow mucus or phlegm that smokers cough up regularly.

Moving away from the lungs, smoking harms your heart. Heart disease and stroke are both more likely as a consequence.

Diabetes (where a person cannot regulate their own blood sugar levels) can end in strokes (again), blindness, heart and kidney disease – and an increased risk of diabetes is also attached to smoking too.

On the more superficial level, smoking causes premature aging (causing your good looks to deteriorate more quickly) and problems with stale breath and yellowing skin around the fingers and finger tips can be expected the more you smoke.

Despite all this, smoking is massively addictive. This is because smoking delivers nicotine from tobacco. The University of California San Francisco (UCSF) has published their own findings that

"Nicotine has been proven to be as addictive as cocaine and heroin and may even be more addictive."

Now, without question, if you said to most people (regardless of their age) "Would you be willing to dabble in some heroin or cocaine?" they would be sensible enough to say "No". They would probably be quite shocked. *Why?* Because everyone knows that cocaine and heroin are horrendously addictive and harmful to your health.

We know and we accept that frequent use of cocaine and heroin is immediately (that is – in the short term and quite rapidly) more harmful than tobacco and nicotine consumption (which is one of the reasons why cocaine and heroin are illegal drugs). Heroin and cocaine have the addictive qualities that are likely to get a person to develop dependency through only limited use, and then the harms will escalate very quickly.

Smoking has killed more people than covid.

Smoking is highly addictive and – again – this means that even relatively small use can create dependency and addiction problems. The high harms of smoking are cumulative and add up over time, far more slowly than someone who is using heroin or cocaine.

This being said – all the horrible things connected to smoking – the expense, the health problems, the issues that change how you look, feel, smell... they get swept away by the addiction. *That's how addiction operates.* You want just one more cigarette.

Traditionally down the years the tobacco companies would compete with each other to attract young smokers. *Why?* In the simple language of one leaked industry document: 'attrition'. Attrition means 'loss' and in this context, loss means death (death of customers is not a good thing for your business). So as smokers died of smoking related illnesses, big tobacco companies needed new people to start smoking to replace the loss of (dead) customers. *That's pretty cold.*

By the way, the World Health Organisation estimates that around 7 million people have died of smoking related illnesses worldwide (which is equivalent to a global pandemic). 2 million more through 'passive smoking' (breathing second hand smoke).

The name given to the tobacco industry is 'Big Tobacco'. 'Big Tobacco' knows that once a person develops a taste for a brand it is unlikely that they will trade that brand in (people are strangely brand loyal to addictive substances). Marketing to people in their 30s or 40s is nearly pointless. *You need to get young people to smoke, and you need to get them to smoke your brand.*

As a consequence, through the 1950s, the 1960s and forward from there into more recent times – we saw advertising that denied or minimised the health implications of smoking, and associated smoking brands with sports, with vibrant young people who looked a little bit more 'grown-up', and even with cartoon characters in Saturday morning TV shows.

One of the biggest scandals involved a piece of media released by several tobacco companies jointly that was called 'A Frank Statement to Cigarette Smokers' and it was released on 4th January 1954 in the United States.

Within the many claims, one of the direct assurances was 'there is no proof that cigarette smoking causes cancer' (there was plenty of evidence) and it even promised that the tobacco industry would 'cooperate closely' with public health agencies to safeguard public health (the industry did not).

It has since been shown categorically that the companies that run the tobacco industry (currently worth close to $1 trillion US dollars worldwide) conspired

"...creating doubt about the health charge without actually denying it."

At the same time the industry worked relentlessly to make the consequences of smoking the fault of the consumer (their customers) and not their poisonous product.

Unsurprisingly as more was revealed about the impact smoking has on personal health, and the tighter the regulations became around how smoking could be advertised, smoking *did* indeed begin to fall into decline. The value of the global tobacco market fell steadily year on year from the beginning of the 2010s until around 2017 – when something changed everything about that trend. That something was *vaping*.

Vaping has been announced – *it has been agreed almost universally* – as the healthier alternative to smoking. This being said we do have to apply some realism to that announcement.

Nicotine is still a toxin (poison) to humans. Vaping is still a flavoured delivery method of the toxin that is nicotine.

The nicotine that is delivered from vaping is the same addictive product that was delivered through cigarettes. This means that once they have you as a customer, you will feel compelled to keep buying their product. At the moment vaping is cheaper than smoking – but the majority of cost involved in smoking is taxation. In fact, the tax on cigarettes is 16.5% PLUS £5.26 added to every packet of 20 cigarettes. So if a packet of cigarettes is about £15 almost half of that cost is taken by the government in tax. The more people switch to vaping the more taxation is likely to be directed by the government at that addictive product too.

The vaping outlets will tell you that at the moment vaping is 93% cheaper than smoking 20 cigarettes per day[36]. Earlier in this chapter we estimated that 20 cigarettes per day was going to cost you in the region of £5475 per year (if you don't roll your own). So the suggestion is that vaping to the same extent would cost something like £380 per year –

---

[36] 'Vape-simple.com'

roughly £32 per month. This is far from being 'cheap' – *in fact it's enough to get you a decent mobile phone contract.*

This isn't what troubles me about vaping so much though. What troubles me about vaping is that, as a product, vaping has helped the tobacco industry to recover it's fortunes. An industry that looked like it was destined to fall into decline (and deserved to fall into decline, having killed several million people). Tobacco is now set to reach a worth of about $1 trillion dollars in the next 3 years[37] and the decline of the world tobacco market has rallied by more than $80 billion US dollars worldwide since vaping was introduced in 2017.

At the height of the smoking boom the tobacco companies were assuring customers that their product wasn't provably linked to cancer, couldn't be proven to be harmful to health, they even marketed it with doctors and dentists, and they sold it as a positive, fashionable lifestyle choice. It turned out to be a death causing global crisis of addiction that the World Health Organisation has had to respond to.

Now the same people want you to trust them that – no seriously this time – vaping is *not* bad for you. The loophole that they weave through of course is that they are now helping people to 'stop smoking' and there is a lot of agreement at this stage that vaping is not as bad as smoking (at least, the evidence at the moment suggests as much). I would caution you - there are a lot of things that are better

---

[37] Statista

for you than smoking that I wouldn't recommend as healthy. You have to keep some perspective on just how poisonous and harmful smoking is, it's one of the very worst lifestyle health choices that you can possibly make!

All we know about vaping is that we haven't seen the long-term impacts and we don't have the data to know conclusively what is going to happen to a generation who are starting to vape now. Personally - I don't trust tobacco companies and I don't think they have a track record of valuing their customers or having their best interests at heart. As industries go – there are few that have been as bad when it comes to literally killing their own customers.

Vaping is presented as cool and adult – much as smoking was when I was growing up in the 1980s and 1990s. Today it's the same image but a different product. You have to make up your own mind. You do have to be mindful of the fact that possession of a vape, and vaping in school is likely to attract a quite serious sanction though[38].

Drugs

Ok so let's talk about drugs. In my previous section on smoking I said that smoking is one of the worst lifestyle choices that you can possibly make. Why did I say 'one of'? *Well*... drugs!

---

[38] Many schools operate fixed term exclusions.

First of all, there are all manner of drugs. We live in a chemical world, and we all use drugs. It's probably more accurate to actually talk about 'psychoactive substances'. *What on earth does that mean?* Well 'psycho' doesn't mean someone who is going crazy – although it often gets used in that context. 'Psycho' means 'your brain' – as in 'psychological' (which is about the way you think). 'Active' is pretty easy. It means it triggers an effect on your brain. So we are talking about substances that trigger an effect in your brain. Generally, we do know and accept that if a substance triggers an effect in your brain it will also have a physical effect on your body too.

When people talk about 'drugs', naturally they think about things like cannabis ('weed') or cocaine or MDMA ('ecstasy'). These things are all illegal – but there are lots of *legal* psychoactive substances too, and we need to be mindful of what they can do.

One of the most common of the harmful legal substances is paracetamol. The average dose of paracetamol for an adult is two 500mg tablets. Commonly you might take paracetamol when you have a headache or you have a cold and it offers mild pain relief. The mild pain relief makes us think that it's a pretty harmless substance, but the lethal dose of paracetamol can be as few as twelve tablets and it is recommended that nobody should take more than four doses of two tablets in a 24 hour period. When I was a police officer the vast majority of suicide attempts in girls were made by taking an overdose of paracetamol – it's easy to get hold of and there is a perception that because it's a pain killer the route to death will be logically pain free. I have been advised by doctors that paracetamol kills because it damages vital organs and it is an exceptionally painful way to take a life.

Caffeine is a psycho-active substance that comes within the category of 'stimulants'. These type of 'drugs' give you energy and wake you up or keep you awake. Caffeine is commonly in coffee, sometimes in tablet form, and of course, energy drinks are also loaded with caffeine too. Caffeine, like a lot of stimulants, creates tolerance – that is, your body gets used to it so you generally need a bit more to get the same 'kick' out of it. An over use of caffeine can create dependency too. So if you've been drinking a lot of coffee over a long time, and you suddenly stop, you're going to feel a bit rubbish for a while. Again, this might include low mood, being irritable, feeling very tired and generally out of sorts. I am terrible for drinking too much coffee and this is a perfect example of where someone might say "I don't use drugs" – ok, well actually...

Cannabis is an important thing to know about. The availability of cannabis has increased massively in local communities and the business model ('County Lines') surrounding the supply of illegal drugs and cannabis specifically is exceptionally dangerous to young people (in fact I've written other books about it).

So, cannabis is something that I would advise is highly problematic on two levels. First of all, cannabis is thought of as a soft, harmless drug that is unlikely to create addiction or dependency. The effect of being 'high' on cannabis is thought of as being gentle and quite sociable. All of these perceptions persuade people that weed is not a problem and it's not a big deal if you get into it. This is a bit of a 'wolf in sheep's clothing' (a hidden threat) – that is to say, it's not like that at all.

Cannabis is made of two specific chemicals that influence strength and purity – these two chemicals are cannabidiol (CBD) and (long word) tetrahydrocannabinol (THC).

Stay with me here folks. It is the THC that has an impact on the brain. The more THC there is, the stronger the weed is.

Psychosis is a clinical term for 'mental illness'.

THC is classed as a 'psychotic' – that is, it causes 'psychosis'. 'Psychosis' is (strictly speaking) a category of mental illness, and is used to describe how people lose contact with the reality around them or can't engage with it clearly. This might involve seeing or hearing things that aren't real. It might involve having panic attacks for no reason. Equally it can involve bursting into laughter and finding things hysterically funny when there is nothing going on to cause that.

While THC causes temporary psychosis or psychotic symptoms (effects) long term use of THC means that the brain is more likely to develop long term problems with psychosis, whether the user is smoking cannabis or not. For this reason THC is illegal.

CBD is the opposite to THC in many ways – it is an *anti-psychotic*. We don't use it medically because medical science has discovered and created more effective ways of treating psychosis – but nevertheless CBD is recognised as an anti-psychotic, it is legal, and it tends to make people feel relaxed, drowsy or less stressed. There has been a huge increase in shops selling CBD products and oils as a home remedy for people to use. How effective it is, well that's open to question.

In cannabis the THC and the CBD traditionally balance against each other – and in years gone by cannabis had a bit more THC, and a little bit less CBD, to create an interesting overall effect on the human brain.

So it might be 5% THC and 3% CBD. *Remember – most drugs entertain or stimulate the brain in some way otherwise the people who use those drugs wouldn't go back to them.* A low level of THC will tickle the brain – whereas a heavier amount of THC will hit the brain harder. More or less CBD will soften that experience or do something to cushion it.

Over the years I spent in the police I saw the street purity levels of weed rise sharply, so the amount of THC went up and up. CBD values, the counterbalance – dropped. Some of this is to do with the way in which the THC rich plants are grown in darkened rooms under UV lights (absolutely none of this stuff is 'organic') and some of it is about how the plant is bred and developed over time.

Today many countries have legalised cannabis and by browsing the international shops and producers online we can learn quite a lot. For example, in such countries as Canada and the USA you can buy your own seeds and grow your own plants. Some of these products offer the 'old school' cannabis experience of lower THC values – but some have alarming names like 'ghost train' or 'amnesia haze' and can offer THC levels that are beyond 25%.

Needless to say – any cannabis product that has a high THC value has a high risk of a psychotic experience attached to it.

The drug itself is a class B illegal drug in the United Kingdom. That means that being in possession of it is unlawful and you can be arrested for it. It also means that supplying it – even giving it away (you don't have to be paid) – is also very much illegal. The people that you buy weed from *are* drug dealers, don't tell yourself that they're not, because they are part of a chain.

In the UK, cannabis is commonly bought from a street level drug dealer. This person rarely knows what the THC value of the drug is and the consistency or reliability of any such product is highly questionable. You cannot know what you're about to use and you simply have to trust the criminal that you bought it from to tell you the truth. Like prohibition alcohol in the United States, it's an unregulated market full of very strong products created in questionable circumstances.

Buying drugs (not just cannabis – but any drug) from a drug dealer brings you into close contact with the wrong type of people. These people are not selling you something to help you to achieve your life goals or aspirations. They do not care about you as a person. They only care about the money. They are likely to encourage you to buy more than you can afford and to 'pay them back'. They might offer you 'free' product to get you hooked in. They want to create debt, addiction and dependency and that's when it can get pretty nasty. You have to keep going back to use more of what they offer, and they can put more and more pressure on you to give them back more money than you 'borrowed'. They might encourage you to sell drugs to 'pay off' whatever debt you got into. This is what we call 'debt bondage' and it's a common form of modern-day slavery.

Cannabis dependency and addiction is a real thing. The rumours that cannabis does not create addiction are false and more and more young people are having to seek support from the National Health Service to treat cannabis dependency problems. CASUS (Child and Adolescent Substance Misuse Services) suggest that 1 in 10 users are reporting problems with addiction and dependency associated with cannabis, and these numbers are more likely to rise in the earlier teenage years.

Cannabis is one of the most common illegal drugs out there. Smoking cannabis does not mean that you will *definitely* graduate into harder drugs like cocaine, ketamine, heroin or the various pills and powders. I don't hold with the 'gateway' argument. That being said, once you start to experiment with cannabis, the risks of you becoming less wary of other drugs is more substantial, and there aren't many heroin addicts out there who didn't get started by softening their attitude to drugs by using cannabis first.

I do tend to support the legalised and controlled distribution of cannabis by the government, if only to take the multi-billion-pound industry out of the hands of organised criminals. Cannabis as a drug is definitely dangerous – particularly dangerous to the developing brains of young people through adolescence – but that has to be considered against the threat that organised crime poses to young people too. Young people are being targeted in a highly aggressive way by organised crime groups and cannabis is a key part of that.

I am not saying that we should legalise cannabis because it is safe, and I definitely do not encourage anyone to try it or to experiment with it. Of all the people I have met with drug problems, the ones who have used cannabis heavily remain the most obvious to me. The long-term impact on the brain can be very telling – long after the user has stopped taking it. Additionally, a major effect of heavy cannabis misuse is a generally hazy, foggy, sleepy, uncaring personal attitude that really stops you from finding your focus, your motivation and your determination to do something positive with your life.

There are a lot of very problematic and dangerous substances out there – legal and illegal. I wanted to focus on cannabis because it is a specific risk to teenagers, and I know that the broad availability of cannabis to young people is incredibly high.

At the end of this book, you'll find a number of resources including advice on what to do if you feel you might have developed a problem with cannabis, if you are worried for a friend, or if you need help with any other drug or substance.

Alcohol should always be taken seriously. The more you drink the more vulnerable you become.

Smoking is expensive and poisonous. I don't trust vaping either.

You can get more information on drugs by visiting 'talktofrank.com'

Alcohol, Smoking & Drugs

Checklist:

- Addiction and dependency can happen to anyone.
- Addiction and dependency are life-long problems and there is no 'cure' for addiction.
- Alcohol kills more than 9,000 people per year in the United Kingdom.
- Drinking lowers natural inhibitions and makes a drinker more vulnerable to risks taking behaviours.
- Drinking can compromise a person's ability to give true consent to sex.
- Smoking is regarded by the World Health Organisation to be a global epidemic.
- Smoking is expensive, poisonous, causes premature aging and in the UK it is illegal to smoke indoors in a public venue.
- There hasn't been enough research conducted into vaping to know whether it is a safe long-term pastime or not.
- 'Drugs' are a label that we apply to things that change how you think, feel and behave.
- You can look up individual drugs by visiting **www.talktofrank.com**
- Cannabis is often mistaken for a safe or non-addictive substance. In truth there is a lot more to cannabis than is hidden in the popular reputation.
- Drugs are generally illegal to buy and sell. If you're buying drugs you're putting yourself in contact with criminal organisations either directly or indirectly.

Chapter 11:
Mental Health

As you get older you come to realise that your mental health and wellbeing is absolutely everything. It is the foundation of your ability to enjoy life and to achieve the things that you aim for. Without good mental health you can be in the most beautiful place on earth – on a holiday in the most exotic and perfect location – *and you can still feel awful.*

Mental health, much like your physical health, is a balance. You will find that keeping yourself engaged and stimulated with *enough* stress (so that you find what you are doing to be interesting and rewarding) but not *too much* stress – is a tricky thing to manage. Sometimes getting that balance right takes you very close to a level of stress that begins to feel uncomfortable or might even be harmful.

Likewise, you ability to cope with levels of stress will expand and contract based on lots of factors including how tired you feel, whether you are hungry, your physical health and more.

Boredom can be harmful and stressful all on its own. Solitary confinement[39] is a punishment that has been used by countless civilisations through history. You can't just 'switch everything off' and sit in isolation and expect to feel good. The happy place, the sweet spot, sits somewhere in between, and it's a slightly different experience for everyone.

---

[39] A situation where a person is left alone in an empty room with nothing to do and no perception of time.

'Stress' is talked about as a negative thing that happens when we are under too much pressure. There are too many things going on, there is too much to worry about and you begin to feel out of control. In this situation you might have anxiety attacks, the sudden onset of that horrible worrying feeling, and it can bring all kinds of physical symptoms, like feeling sick, or needing to go to the toilet, or headaches.

You might think that having absolutely no stimulation is the *opposite* of stress – *having to do nothing at all* and speak to absolutely nobody. In truth the mind needs a certain amount of engagement to remain healthy and well balanced. It is actually painful to sit and have nothing at all to do. Literally staring at a blank wall – over an extended and prolonged period, becomes inhumane.

Good mental health happens when we successfully balance the spectrum of 'too much stimulation' and 'not enough stimulation' – and we get to a really nice place where, somewhere in between we have 'enough'.

There is a very modern fascination with getting 'as much as possible'. We have a billionaire culture now where 50% of the world's wealth is owned by 1% of the richest people on the planet. We look up to people who consume as much as they can and who do it as conspicuously (as obviously) as they possibly can. People with private jets, big cars, having lots of houses in different parts of the world... and they broadcast all this material wealth on the internet and via social media. People rarely stop to think about the idea of 'balance' or 'need'.

First of all if you own ten houses in different regions of the world, how many can you actually live in at any one time? If you own a fleet of ten luxury cars, how many can you drive at one time? At the heart of all this is the idea that the more you have, and the more you get, the better things are for you and the more successful you have been. *That's the idea anyway.*

Lots of people have written about the emptiness and the loneliness that they experienced when they achieved the dream of material riches. What happens when you suddenly get all this 'stuff' – do you achieve mental wellbeing? Do you suddenly feel satisfied? Someone who advocates a lot on mental health and wellness is the former heavyweight world champion boxer, Frank Bruno. He has made the point that he realised, with all his riches, he could still only wear one pair of trousers, and just like everyone else, he put them on one leg at a time.

In truth, trying to compensate for a lack of happiness or mental health through money and having 'more stuff' is not addressing the problem. You're distracting yourself with shiny things that you *think* are going to make you feel happy.

We've discussed self-awareness and compassion in this book already. We've considered how we fit into a society. For a large period of time the biggest society around you will be your school – that is your first big community. It's where you learn to live in a community. Hopefully it is where you learn to use your talents to improve yourself while you contribute to the community overall.

Self-awareness is critical to your sense of mental stability and your good mental health. This involves learning to live with the balance of being happy in what you do – taking a reasonable consideration for the feelings of others, but not living for their approval or congratulations all the time.

Driving onwards and all the time trying to achieve 'more', might feel like the thing to do, but it really is like setting off on a journey without knowing where you're going. Yes – that's an adventure, and yes, that can be great fun for a while – but as we discussed around your aspirations, there comes a time when you need a destination, and you need to understand what matters to you (what your values are).

It's a cliché (that is 'something that is said again and again') that people get to a certain stage in their life, realise what they have become and they say "This isn't what I wanted to be" or "This isn't what I wanted to turn out like".

In the very worst cases a person might even turn around and say "I've become everything that I hated". In and of itself this might sound like the absolutely worst thing that could happen to you. In honesty, if you have that realisation, at least you know what you *don't want to be as a person*, and logically, you start to realise what you do want to be, as a result of that. There is nothing stopping you, at any stage of your life, from becoming a version of yourself that you genuinely want to be.

Today ships navigate by complicated computers and GPRS systems connected to satellites. In the old days they had to use charts of the stars – and recognising a star meant that they could understand where their ship was, and where they needed to guide it towards. Even if you realise that you are unhappy, simply knowing what makes you unhappy gives you a fixed point (like a star) that you could navigate from. *"Ok – so I know that I don't want to go over there"*.

Striving towards what you *want to be,* can be stressful. First of all, telling people what you want to be and what your goal is, can make you feel insecure. You might fear that they'll laugh at you.

Having people laugh at you is not so bad. Particularly if your ambition is to become a clown...

Setting goals and having standards to perform against naturally causes some anxiety – can I make that level? Can I live up to my own expectations? What will people think of me? What if I fail? For most people the worst critic in their life lives inside their own head. You'll often find that forgiving *yourself* is much harder than forgiving someone else. I have heard lots of people say *"I speak to myself in a way that I would never treat anyone else"*. This is not a sign of good mental health.

Striving against goals to make yourself happy *can* work – certainly there is a sense of achievement – but it doesn't guarantee good mental health. Getting promoted at work for example. Winning a prize. Achieving in exams and building qualifications. These things matter and they have natural benefits and rewards attached to them – but sometimes the source of your mental wellbeing is not connected to such things at all. *"I've achieved all this and I'm still not happy? Why am I not happy?"*. Some people find that they have worked incredibly hard to achieve amazing things – but as soon as they achieve that thing they lose respect for it almost instantly – because they didn't learn to love or appreciate themselves first.

"It can't have been that amazing if I achieved it."

"Well, if I could achieve it, I guess anyone can. So what's special about that?"

In truth this comes down to respect for yourself, love for yourself and admiration of your own personal qualities. What good is going through all the stress, putting in all the hours, beating the challenge – if all is does is prove to yourself that you don't love yourself very much? If you can win a huge prize and still talk to yourself with such disregard, all you've found out is that your real challenge is learning to love and respect yourself.

Some people get to the top of the mountain and they spend that time looking across the amazing view that they have discovered. They have a moment of their own time, a moment that they know won't last forever and they get to gaze down on everything. They know that they might never return there again. It's a beautiful moment, but it's also a painful moment. It's full of what they gained, but it's also full of what they know they also have to lose now (unless they find a way to repeat that achievement). You can't stay there, you can't live in that moment for the rest of your life.

For some, they are consumed with the pain of feeling that it wasn't worth it. What on earth do you do? You might have invested years of hard, stressful work to hold something in your hands – and then you realise that it wasn't what you thought it was going to be? Or that you're going to have to give it back?

In many regards this is because adornments, awards, money and material recognition can be wonderful and enjoyable things – but they don't fill the gap in your mental health if you don't learn to appreciate yourself at the time before all that happens - when you apparently have nothing.

If you don't learn how to love yourself when you have nothing at all – how are you going to love and admire yourself simply because you have all these awards? *What you are loving and admiring are the awards – not yourself.*

Now it may be that you wanted to discover that love and respect of yourself – or give yourself a reason to love and respect yourself. That desire drove you on to achieve things that you felt you could love and respect yourself *for*. It gave you the fuel that you needed to become successful in a way that could be measured and quantified: *"I've won four Grammy awards, two Oscars, a knighthood and I've made £18 million"* – that's a lot of 'winning'. It probably took a lot of hard work too. It helps us to place that person into a particular circle of 'success' (material success) – a context. How does that person feel about themselves though? After all the show business glitz and glamour, they go home and the have to deal with an eating disorder? Body image issues? Self-harm? Problems with drugs? If they hide their true personality?

For many the achievements and awards become a way to mask the fact that they never took the time to accept themselves and learn to love themselves (for all their imperfections) long before they became that movie star, or sports star or successful and wealthy businessperson. For many actors the 'movie star' version of themselves is as much a role they play as any character that they depict on the screen in a film.

Pete Sampras was the incredible tennis champion who won no fewer than 64 major career titles including seven Wimbledon titles. In a career that lasted 14 stunning years he simply won everything. Sampras redefined winning in tennis and how dominant one professional could be. He was jealously characterised in the media as a boring, robotic tennis machine that ground down his opponents and won. Pete Sampras opened the door to a new era of tennis – for the likes of Roger Federer, Rafa Nadal and Novak Djokovic – who took his longevity and athleticism to a new inspired level that shares the same type of determination and professionalism. Aside from anything, Pete Sampras was a sublime tennis player who mastered all aspects of the game and few opponents ever saw a weakness in how he played.

Despite all of this – and the millions of dollars that he earned in prizes and endorsements (multiples sources suggest that he is worth around $150 million) – and despite his reputation of being without emotion in how he played and conducted himself – Pete Sampras is indeed human. In his autobiography he admitted that the level of stress, the mental health side of his life, was not what people thought it was. He describes walking off the court and collapsing. Losing handfuls of his hair. He even found a way to attribute his best performances to someone or something else that was imagined. He spoke about 'the gift': When he was young, he realised he was gifted at tennis. When he won he said that it was because he was playing with 'the gift' and that it was 'the gift' that was winning. When he lost, *he felt that it was because he wasn't connected to the gift – and he was playing on his own, just Pete Sampras.*

In truth – Pete Sampras won everything because he trained, practised and honed his talent, was incredibly detailed in his diet and exercise, and devoted everything he had to his craft.

Some people can become so successful that they realise that no matter how much they win or achieve they are never going to be satisfied and it won't make the difference as to whether they learn to love and respect themselves. It doesn't give them mental wellbeing. In a room full of awards and all the accolades they have gained – they realise that they would give it all back just to know how to be kinder to themselves and how to appreciate themselves individually. And be happy.

This chapter is not devoted to telling you that winning things is pointless. It is devoted to telling you that winning things is pointless *if all it does is cause you pain.*

What you need to do, from an early stage, is encourage yourself to be ambitious, aim for the great results and outcomes that you genuinely and truly deserve – *but be ready to understand and appreciate yourself no matter if you are winning or losing.*

Mohammed Ali was an icon – but before he even won his first title – when his name was still 'Cassius Clay' – he was already telling people

"I am *the* greatest"

In fact, a term that is common now, 'GOAT' – 'Greatest of All Time', was coined by Ali. He didn't just say "I am the greatest in this moment" – he was the greatest, he was always the greatest (forever), and he wanted everyone to know that he always would be the greatest. It was utterly and completely unconditional.

Did he ever lose? Well yes, as a matter of fact, he did. He lost five very painful times (there is no other way to lose in boxing – if you get beaten in boxing you don't just get beaten, you get *beaten up*). In the case of one defeat Ali had his jaw broken in the second round of the fight and carried that injury until he finished the full duration of the 12 rounds losing on points in a painful split decision to Ken Norton (who carried on punching him in the face through the fight of course). Even when Ali won, some of his victories were won through hugely painful and prolonged contests. No matter what – he had to go back to his dressing room (or to the hospital) and he had to find that self-love and admiration that helped him to put himself back together and carry on. *I cannot imagine that you feel like 'the greatest' when you've just lost and you have a broken jaw.*

Winning things is fantastic – and you can go through all kinds of pain barriers and stress barriers to get there. Doing it with self-love and a care for your mental health and wellbeing is so much more of an achievement though. Self-love does not mean self-indulgence, doing whatever you want, spoiling yourself all the time, avoiding the things that you don't like doing. Self-love also means building the resilience to take on big challenges, to believe in yourself when other people do not, and being able to still love yourself when you do or don't reach the aim or the goal that you set for yourself.

Walt Whitman is a great American poet from the 19th century. He was a visionary who wrote about the future of America when the country was still evolving. He wrote about finding a sense of identity. He wrote a lot about courage:

"Have you heard that it was good to gain the day?
I also say it is good to fall, battles are lost in the same spirit in which they are won[40]."

Here Whitman acknowledges that it's not always about winning. You learn and gain so much from an apparent defeat – but more than anything else, sometimes you did your best, and on that particular day you can be proud of that, despite the fact that you didn't 'win' in the ultimate outcome.

Having the balance of treating success and failure in the same even-handed way is important – never too carried away with success, never too crushed by the defeat. Another poet, Rudyard Kipling famously wrote:

"If you can meet with Triumph and Disaster

---

[40] Walt Whitman – 'Song of Myself' (1855)

And treat those two imposters just the same[41];"

You see – of both triumph (winning) or disaster (failing) – neither of them are *you*. They are both imposters, and people are sometimes deceived and tricked into thinking of you by your successes and failures. In doing so they never see the reality of who you actually are. Treating both outcomes the same, even if one is a much happier experience, the other more painful, but also knowing that neither of them are 'you', is critically important. We never let that unsettle our emotional or our mental good health, our sense of balance – as difficult sometimes as that might be.

Good mental health is built from a solid foundation of knowing yourself and being kind to yourself – not pretending that you are perfect – but learning to love your imperfections. Working hard to improve on what you don't do well, working hard to make the most of your natural gifts and talents is important. Never being arrogant or getting carried away with those things, never being too alarmed, anxious or distressed about your weaknesses either. These are signs of good mental health.

Working hard to establish this as your foundation – and return to this when you are in the big moments is genuinely hard. Remind yourself that this is where you work from, this is who you *really* are, no matter whether it's a successful

---
[41] Rudyard Kipling – 'If' (1895)

moment or a moment that caused you disappointment – this is who you will continue to be.

So we know that finding balance and self-love, with not too much stress, nor too little – promotes good mental health.

We know that not becoming preoccupied with the idea of success, or allowing accolades or money to define you will help you to deal with both the arrival of success, or the lack of success and of course, the arrival of disappointment.

We know that having an honest understanding of yourself – your strengths and weaknesses – with a proper appreciation of your gifts and talents (we all have them) – will help to promote a realistic sense of self love and personal regard.

We know that not allowing success to go to your head nor defeat or loss to destroy your self-confidence is absolutely important to being able to keep you moving forward.

All of these things are fundamental[42] (long term) to the foundation of whatever it is that you want to build. *No matter what you want to do or who you want to be.*

What are the other things that you can do – in the short term – that will help you to promote your mental health and wellbeing?

In the short term, there are tactics and tools that help you to get back to that balanced sense of who you are. Such things help you individually to get back to that place of balance and stability when you feel you are in a crisis.

---

[42] Of the highest importance

Knowing your triggers

First of all – know your 'triggers'. Triggers are the things that, when they are sprung, they propel you in a certain direction. They have a particular outcome that you don't necessarily feel in control of. When someone touches a 'trigger' there is a likelihood – a very high likelihood – that you are going to respond in a specific way. That specific way might not be healthy or positive one (very often, it is not). With someone who suffers from addiction it might result in a relapse.

Everyone has different triggers and I spend a lot of time with young people trying to identify what they are. If we know what our triggers are we can either avoid them (when they happen repeatedly in the same circumstances) or we can recognise them before or even while they are happening – so that we remind ourselves not to fall into the trap of doing that negative thing.

Let me give you some common examples – I will use 'quotes' that are very similar to the things that I have been told directly. Usually these are about behaviour in the classroom:

"When he [teacher] talks to me disrespectfully. I'm not just gonna take that. He can't do that to me in front of everyone. I *hate* him."

"I will not be told what to do. I won't. You can't tell me what to do. They're not *God*. They are not my boss."

"When it's not fair. And they won't listen. Everyone was talking – everyone – and I got singled out for it. It's *always* me."

"I found out that they were chatting **** about me on SnapChat. What am I supposed to do?"

Not everyone is triggered by this stuff – but many people are. The same stuff happens all the time in schools up and down the country.

Sure – I absolutely agree – if the teacher's tone was always soft and diplomatic it might help, but sometimes they do need to be more direct (because students can be rude), and when they're not, sometimes they're having a bad day too (remember – teachers are humans). Maybe you'd prefer if they said:

"I'd really appreciate it if you could do me a favour and sit here – I'd be really grateful"

Rather than:

"James Smith –you've been warned, that's enough! Sit over there!"

But ask yourself honestly – if the teacher does take that milder tone with you, do you always reward it by actually cooperating? Some people mistake that kindness for weakness and try to exploit it by pushing the boundaries.

The tone they have adopted might seem disrespectful to you – they might be telling you what to do (they might need to). It happens to everyone at some time. In a situation where we know our triggers we can either avoid that (I had one boy tell me "I used to go to play football for Coalforth Rangers [not a real team] – but the coach just ordered us around and talked to us a certain way – so I moved to Sawbridge FC [again, not real] and I'm happier now") or we find a way to deal with that moment and release that tension in a more controlled way (either there and then or later on).

Some of the young people I work with have 'exit cards' and they go and stand outside of the classroom for five minutes to just let themselves calm down a little bit because they are more sensitive to such triggers than other students.

When it comes to talking – and 'everyone is doing it' – and you feel that you are consistently punished or sanctioned? On one level, you have to admit that if everyone else if talking it doesn't make your talking ok. The mistake the teacher is making is not in sanctioning you – *it's in not sanctioning others too*. Do you want to help the teacher out by pointing out your friends? It's not a happy situation – but it's one you have to learn to manage. Above all else – it's one that you have to take responsibility for. One simple coping tactic in this situation is not being one of the people who talk in that class. Don't be talking in *that* class – you know that this teacher won't tolerate it (some teachers tolerate talking more than others).

You might not like this advice – but give it a try and see how much better things get? If it really upsets you that much, perhaps you could talk to your teacher about moving to a seat where you are less likely to talk and if the group talk continues it will be obvious that it wasn't all about you (particularly if you're not talking in your new seat).

If what is upsetting you is that you want to sit with your friends and talk in class – well I can't help you with that, you know that's not going to work. *Be honest with yourself*.

People gossiping about you online? Have you ever gossiped online about other people and their business? I bet that you have. Did you think about how it felt for that other person? We have discussed empathy and compassion already. Whether you like it or not, social media encourages a gossip culture. You also participate in that – or there is a very high likelihood that you have.

"I didn't think that person would find out"

Well they did. Flipping that situation around – you found out that people were gossiping about you online and you didn't like what got said.

You have two options – do something about it *or let it slide*. If you do something about it, you either get it resolved by someone else, or you do your best to resolve it personally. We've looked at conflict de-escalation. I advise you to report the matter to a trusted adult, blocking the people involved, and moving on. Don't take it into your own hands and don't turn it into a feud or beef (as we have discussed elsewhere). Remember that being on social media is a choice.

What we are talking about in all these situations is having a plan – a contingency (remember our previous chapter). "I *know that when this happens, it upsets me. I know how likely it is that such things will happen"*. In a calm moment we come up with a way to deal with it – and when it happens we stick to the plan. This helps you to stay calm, promotes your sense of control and balance, and gets you back to the big picture of your own welfare as soon as possible. **This is what is genuinely important for your mental wellbeing.**

Just as important as 'knowing your triggers' – you should know the things that also work to calm you down and make you feel good again.

This is the opposite of knowing your angry triggers – in a way these are different triggers, happiness triggers. Things that make you feel much better about yourself and give you a moment of time that is peaceful and more supportive.

This can include knowing who to speak to. We all have one person that we can go to for advice and reassurance – and that person gives good calm wisdom that doesn't amplify your anxiety or your negative thoughts.

Having something to eat or drink – and knowing *what* to eat and what to drink. For example, eating something packed with sugar and caffeine probably won't help you to calm down. Some foods are described as 'comfort foods' and while I don't encourage you to go and empty the fridge when you feel insecure – you might find that having a sensible bite to eat, and maybe a cup of tea – and a moment of rest while you do that, makes you feel a lot better. Sometimes life gets so busy and stressful that we forget to eat. We get dehydrated. We get 'hangry' (hungry plus angry).

Going to a particular place can make you feel better, safer and more secure. There might be a place in the school that you like to sit. A window that you like to look out of. Somewhere warm and quiet. Maybe in the library. Personally I always found the school library to be one of the calmest rooms in the building.

Don't sit in the school toilets when you're upset. It might seem private but it looks suspicious and people can misunderstand.

There can be other things – lots of other private things – but making a little mental list of them gives you things to do when you're feeling down or when times seem tough.

This chapter on mental health is by no means intended to express a conclusive and full guide to dealing with the complicated picture of mental and emotional distress. I do hope that it gives you a way to understand that we all have mental health – we all have ups and down in our mental health – and we would all benefit from understanding our individual mental health better (including the things that make a situation feel better or make a situation feel worse). You can definitely learn more about this subject and I would encourage you to try.

When I'm feeling low I always turn to my best friend and he makes me feel better!

Oh thanks mate! That's so nice!

My best friend is my dog Pugsy!

Mental Health

Checklist:

- Stress is not a 'bad thing' but too much stress can be.
- Avoiding stress and having no stimulation can be harmful and cause problems.
- Achieving material goals can make you feel happy, but if you don't love yourself before you achieve them, you are unlikely to love yourself *because* you achieved them.
- Learning to love yourself is an important part of your mental health.
- You will experience success and failure at different times in your life, but neither of them are 'you'.
- Find the triggers that make you angry or unhappy. Formulate reliable ways to cope in a more constructive and positive way.
- Find the happy triggers in your life that help you to feel better and restore a sense of calm and peace.
- Find a place in your school where you can sit and feel calm and safe.

Chapter 12:
Every single day counts

Rounding off the book, and I hope that you've enjoyed reading it and that it has proven to be useful to you, I want to talk to you about something that is very important but also very difficult to get your head around! *Every day counts.* **Every single day.**

On the face of it that could seem obvious. A lot can happen in a day. Someone will go out and buy a lottery ticket today and that lottery ticket will win the jackpot prize. Their life will never be the same again. Another person will meet with an accident – perhaps they'll fall off a ladder or down the stairs – and they might be injured in a way that changes their life permanently.

You never know what a day will bring to you – or what is coming around the next corner. All you really know is that your day has twenty-four hours in it. They might tick by, minute by minute and second by second, much as the previous day did. You can never get that time back. You cannot earn it back. You cannot beg for it again. There is nothing that can be done about a day that got beyond you, got away from you, that you didn't make something of.

If you were alive in 2009, you would have been around when something exceptional happened. The kind of quiet event that many people do not remember and didn't realise was happening at the time at all. The first of the major crypto-currencies was born – Bitcoin. When it was released, you could buy an entire Bitcoin for just five pence (5p). For every £1 you would have 20 Bitcoin. For every £10, you'd have 200 Bitcoin. For £100 you would have 2000 Bitcoin. *"So what?"* you might think. Well the price of Bitcoin (at the time of writing) peaked at *$67,566* per coin back in 2021. Or something like £54,000. That's per coin. For anyone who was lucky enough, far sighted enough or for whatever reason decided to buy £100 worth of Bitcoin in 2009 – well in April 2021 (12 years later) that £100 investment would have been worth *£5.4 million*. I think you might definitely remember the day that you bought £5.4 million worth of Bit-Coin for £100.

The world is full of amazing and unlikely possibilities that sneak past you every day. Most of them you simply don't see or recognise. Thomas Jefferson was an American statesman, a Founding Father of his country, and the third President of the United States of America. He said:

"I am a great believer in *luck*, and I find the harder I work, the more I have of it!"

This is *absolutely* true. I also find this to be highly reliable: None of the great men and women of history ever made their name through letting the day pass them by. We have talked in this book about your goals, your ambition – your destination on the journey of your life. **You do not make it to your destination by parking your car at the side of the road and eating sandwiches.**

While it would be nice to buy the winning lottery ticket, or make that Bitcoin purchase – *such things are unlikely* – if we're being honest. But the journey that you take to your goals is based on your ability to attack every single day like it is a meaningful step towards your future.

You only get those 24 hours – and you need to use eight of them for sleep! While you probably won't sleep in the other 16 that are left, you will do other things – you will eat, you will rest in other ways. In terms of the productive length of a day – I would be surprised if you had eight or nine hours to make the very best of. *Twelve hours at an absolute push!*

Being the best at what you want to be takes repetition and practise. Great professionals practise until they can perform with their eyes closed. They dream about what they do. They literally do it in their sleep. Musicians, sports people, crafts people who make things, builders, painters, artists... they hone (carefully sharpen) their abilities. They visualise (imagine) what they are doing. Earlier in this book we discussed the masterful work of the Japanese swordsmiths – investing years in making and perfecting their skills. Their investment is made with small deposits of time, one day at a time. Each day broken into hours. Each hour broken into minutes, like saving pennies in a jar. They know, no matter what the immediate outcome of saving that penny (just another penny) might be, in the long term, that investment is going to add up to something worthwhile.

Remember what we discussed in our chapter about setting a positive routine?

Positive routine turns every day into an opportunity to build something great – and believe me – when it begins to come together, there aren't enough hours in the day. You get to the end of the day, and you look at what you have done with frustration because you know what you wanted it to be, and it isn't there yet. You haven't got there, and you want it to be just right! You don't have time to waste, you don't want to see that precious time being eaten up sitting in a traffic jam, or waiting for a bus that is late, or struggling when the internet goes down, or when something else gets in the way. *You cannot believe that other people aren't moving with the same urgency as you are.*

Your state of mind – *and remember everything that we have said about having good mental health* – dictates exactly what you are going to become. Your ability to visualise what you want to achieve really makes the difference as to whether you can go out there and get it for *real*.

Every day should be an exercise in self-belief. The idea being that the harder you work towards your goals and your dreams, the more things around you begin to move into place.

I don't believe that some kind of mystical energy works in your favour – I just think that as you become more connected to your goal and more focused on your aim – you start to recognise opportunities that you never saw before. Your subconscious mind, that part of your brain that is always ticking over, is more likely to throw up a great idea. You suddenly see something that was always there, *all along*, and you realise "I can use that!". You might even think "I can't believe I never realised that before!". Eureka!

You may have heard the phrase 'Eureka!' (pronounced something like 'your-e-car' – I guess depending on your personal accent). It is supposed to have come from the Greek mathematician Archimedes[43]. He got into the bath one day and saw the water level rise. For whatever reason, in that single moment, he realised that he could accurately measure the volume of an irregular shape. Take a container with a regulated volume of liquid in it, drop the object in, and measure the increase in the total volume. That increase is the volume of the object! Eureka! How many times had Archimedes got into the bath and not realised this? It was a major mathematical breakthrough in problem solving!

You have to convince yourself that you can, before anyone will believe that you will.

---

[43] He died about 200 years before Jesus Christ was born.

Investing positive energy in self-belief, in convincing yourself that you can achieve your dreams and your goals is *never* a waste of time. **You have to convince yourself that you *can*, before anyone else will ever become convinced that you *will*.** You convince yourself that you can, by attacking every single day – and no matter how you come out of that day, you never let the day get the better of you. Trust me. There are some days that will test your resolve and you have to get through them kicking and screaming inwardly.

One day you will do something that surprises you. You'll see the outcomes and you'll think "Wow! I did that!".

It is difficult to imagine your heroes before they were famous – before they were known for their success. Some names have become so incredibly powerful that their success now looks like it was inevitable (that is – nothing could stop it and it was always going to happen). In truth for every champion that is out there, there will be at least ten others that would happily take that champion's place. A champion must train and prepare constantly knowing that someone out there is willing to work just as hard – *or work harder* – to be better than they are. The best dancer, the best athlete, the greatest poet or play-write. *Don't believe me?*

Do you think that the first thing a greater writer ever wrote was of the same incredibly quality as their most successful piece? They worked and worked through mental and emotional pain to get there – to realise the dream of expression through language that really conveyed their thoughts and ideas in a way that made them proud and excited.

Before he died (at the age of 89), the great artist Michelangelo (for some the greatest sculptor that ever lived) spent time literally burning and destroying work that he had done, that he felt did not measure up to the standard that he set for himself later in his life. He was fearful that after his death the people who had worshiped his talents and gifts would find this work and realise that he was just a flawed human being, or that he might be remembered for his lessor creations, instead of his most amazing contributions. Today those priceless pieces of work would be treasured – they would help us to understand the journey that a person goes on in their quest to perfect their passion. In truth Michelangelo *was* a person. He was once a child. He played with other children. He grew up in a certain amount of hardship after his father's business failed. His mother died when he was only six years old. He lived with a nanny and her husband who happened to be a stonecutter. In this tough background Michelangelo found his opportunity to cut marble, and sculpt figures and small statues... Would anyone who met that simple boy realise then, in 1481 (at 6 years old), that he would be remembered and revered in history – hundreds of years later? There are plenty of people who claimed that he was touched by God and by destiny (that he had a certain and decided future) as a special child. One thing is sure – Michelangelo was a simple person who enjoyed his own company, and who lived in his work, invested every day with passion in becoming the best at what he did. He worked to expand what people thought was possible from sculpted stone. When asked how he could possibly create what he had carved he famously said

"I saw the angel in the marble and carved until I set him free."

In a raw piece of marble, a slab, a huge chunk of incredibly heavy rock from the earth, taken from a quarry, he saw the lightness and the divine, heavenly quality of an angel.

My question to you is this: if you are both the slab of marble, and the sculptor, what can you see in yourself? What can you make of yourself?

If one man can see the vision of an angel in a lump of stone – and then turn that lump of stone into the angel that he saw (a lump of stone!) surely you can see the endless potential in yourself? No matter what your background or circumstances? There is nothing less like the wings of an angel, than solid rock that is taken from the ground. The two things are completely opposite. You might see yourself like that rock, you might find it hard to believe that there is an angel inside of you, but it is first your belief and your vision that makes your transformation possible. It is your dedication to every single day that makes it *happen*.

Every day counts on the journey of your development.

There is no room for wasted time in unnecessary conflict, confrontation or feuding with people. Disagreements will come along the way – but you must navigate your way through them to preserve your time and stay focused on your goals.

There is not enough time to hand yourself over to alcohol, smoking, or experimenting aimlessly with harmful drugs.

You might have heard it said that using drugs inspired creative people. A number of extremely talented people have been linked to using drugs – including hallucinogenic drugs (the type of drugs that make you see and hear things that are not real). I prefer to take the word of a lady that I think you might not know if you are in school today. This lady is called Carole King. She was born in 1942 in New York City. She has a rare and incredible gift for music. In her lifetime she has written 118 songs that reached the Billboard Hot 100 in the US, and 61 songs that made the pop charts in the UK. Between 1962 and 2005, Carole King was the most successful female songwriter in the UK singles charts. Period. For an entire 43 years period, she was the best.

Carole King began by writing music for other people to perform. This gave way to her writing music and performing it herself. In 1971 she released an incredible, beautiful album, called 'Tapestry' – a collection of 12 songs which stayed at the top of the US album chart for 15 weeks and remained on the US album charts for the next *six years*. It was – and still is – a masterpiece. This album sold 30 million copies worldwide going platinum 14 times in the US, 8 times in Australia, twice in the UK and 25 times in total, globally.

In her autobiography, her own written recollection of her life[44] she recalled that during the time she spent living in the highly creative environment of California and the hills of Laurel Canyon, Los Angeles, she was introduced to cannabis. She smoked it with other musicians, and they made music that, at the immediate time she was high, she thought sounded incredible. They recorded it as they played. When she listened to it again without the drugs involved, she thought it sounded horrible (and refused to use the music she had made). What she identified was that the drug could twist her perception of what sounded great – but it couldn't make good music. Drugs couldn't magic up some creativity or give her something that wasn't already there when she was sober. In fact, it only seemed to detract from what she had spent years crafting, training, and developing with such care and love. At 80 years old, thankfully Carole King is still with us.

It's not particularly fashionable, I guess, to say that the time wasted on drugs is entirely destructive. If evidence were needed, you don't need to look much further than another great musical woman. Someone – in my opinion – of equal genius to Carole King (there aren't many musicians of that grade). Amy Winehouse was born in 1983 but died tragically at the age of 27. Her passing was mourned deeply and today her singing voice is regarded in the same category as the greatest female jazz and pop vocalists of the modern musical era. She is compared (in terms of her talents and

---

[44] 'A Natural Woman' – Virago, 2013

gifts) to the equally tragic Billie Holiday and the amazing Ella Fitzgerald.

There's a bronze statue of Amy Winehouse in Camden Town, London.

Billie Holiday died in 1959 at the age of 44 (losing her own battle with drugs), Ella Fitzerald died in 1996 (aged 79). Amy Winehouse was a singer who seemed more suited to their era and was inspired by their work – but she broke through with it in 2003/2004. Her sound was jazzy, was soaked in the blues, was multiracial and seemed to give a rebirth to an older world of sounds and tones. Her tastes, her talents, and her gifts – as a performer, as a song writer and as a recording artist were colossal and unique. She was timeless. She sparked a whole new enthusiasm for that smoky sound of the 1940s and 1950s. She took that music and reinvigorated it, infused it with something undoubtedly modern and new. It was music that was gritty, dark and at times harsh, sometimes even violent – but always beautiful. She was recognised at the Brit awards, Ivor Novello awards and the Grammy awards. Her album 'Back to Black' sold 16 million copies worldwide – going platinum 14 times in the UK and twice in the US. She was a beautiful, wonderful, gifted young woman.

Amy Winehouse lost her battle with alcohol and drugs in July 2011. At just 27 years old, and with so much still to give, she was found dead at home following many years of drug and alcohol abuse. Her cause of death was written as being that of 'misadventure' and alcohol poisoning. She is remembered for her lyrics:

"They tried to make me go to rehab

But I said no, no no."

In the end, Amy Winehouse had far *fewer* days than she ought to have had. We treasure everything that she gave us, but we are left to regret that we will never hear any of the music she didn't get time to write and produce in the later years of a life that was stolen from her by drugs and drink.

Count all your days. They are so precious.

My advice to you?

Appreciate your teachers and the time that you have with them. Trust me, at least one of them will be completely unforgettable and you'll never get that time with them again. Never be afraid to show your teachers the appreciation that they deserve for supporting and educating you.

Expect to make mistakes. Try hard to do your best, but you will make mistakes. Every mistake is an independent lesson, *if you take the time to contemplate where that mistake was made, and how you made it.* Don't dwell on those mistakes, don't beat yourself up for those mistakes, but learn from them. Mistakes should keep you modest, and modesty is an excellent quality to stay close to. To expect perfection of yourself is not only unreasonable – it's harmful.

Support your mental health and be a friend to yourself. From time to time consider whether you would treat a good friend in the way that you might criticise yourself. Stop and think what you would advise your friend in the difficult position you find yourself. When you do well, don't forget to reward yourself, be proud of your achievements and thank the people around you.

I advise you to stay honest. Sometimes it might feel easier to be dishonest or 'bend the truth', be the person who finds the strength to be an honest person.

Above all, make the very most of every day. Expect the most of every day. Make it deliver the very best for you.

I'm just like Michelangelo!

Not that Michelangelo Jez!

Every single day counts

Checklist

- The next twenty-four hours might just change your life;
- Every day is significant and if you don't try, you won't find out;
- The harder you work, the luckier you get!
- You are the stone and you are the sculptor. What are you going to carve?
- A lifetime can be short or long – but you don't know!
- Learn from your mistakes, allow them to keep you modest, but don't dwell on them or allow them to undermine you;
- Don't expect perfection from yourself;
- Be a friend to yourself no matter what;
- Be honest and protect your honesty;
- Go out to make the most of every day;

Postscript

I have worked with countless young people over the last four years in a number of very different schools and we've all be through an awful lot.

Facing adolescence through a global pandemic, and perhaps through personal factors that might include bereavement, poverty, having to act as a young carer for parents or siblings – we have to remind ourselves that not all children and young people have the childhood we would want them to enjoy.

In addition to this, organised crime is targeting young people – County Lines, Child Criminal Exploitation, Child Sexual Exploitation and other forms of serious and organised crime have begun to target young people to make huge illegal sums of money. The County Lines drug trade has provoked an increase in serious street-based violence and the carrying of weapons has risen by alarming rates. These are modern phenomena.

When hardship is severe the rewards offered for illegal and criminal behaviours always look more attractive.

If you are one of millions of young people in the UK who have been affected by any of these issues, and you need to reach out for help, you should never suffer in silence.

We have had some incredibly tough times over recent years. *Asking for help is not suggesting that you are failing.*

On the next page I have put together a list of supportive agencies and organisations that you can turn to in all manner of situations.

Take care,

Phil

The following resources might be able to help you:

NHS 101 – call 101 if you have problems with your health or anxieties or worries about your physical or mental wellbeing.

MIND – support mental health for everyone. They have incredible resources to support young people. You can visit their website: www.mind.org.uk you can also call them on 0300 123 3393.

FRANK – independent, impartial and anonymous advice and guidance on drugs. If you need to know more about drugs and substance misuse, call FRANK on 0300 123 6600 or visit www.talktofrank.com. Additionally, FRANK offers anonymous and private 'live chat' (text) online between 2PM and 6PM seven days a week.

The Trussell Trust – the largest provider of foodbank support. If you are struggling to afford food to eat you, are sadly one of many. Visit The Trussell Trust website www.trusselltrust.org and they have a foodbank locator that is easy to use. Many foodbanks also supply essential items like tampons and toiletries too.

The Police – call the police on 111 for a non-emergency issue or visit your local police station. Don't be afraid to go to the police if you have fallen victim of crime. This includes if you recognise the symptoms of abuse that have been inflicted upon you by anyone. Always call 999 in an emergency.

The NSPCC – The biggest charity in the UK supporting children and young people. Their website (www.nspcc.org.uk) has all kinds of excellent resources to help young people stay safe – and this includes online tools for internet safety too.

Childline – Childline has been protecting young people for 35 years. You can call free on 0800 1111. You can visit the website www.childline.org.uk. You can also contact a Childline counsellor via a one-to-one chat room online or through Instagram ('childline_official').

Kooth – is an online mental health and wellbeing community www.kooth.com; You can download their app on your phone or visit them online. They have great tools such as daily mental health journals, online chats with counsellors and discussion boards that are supervised.

Action for Children – www.actionforchildren.org.uk has great support available for young people including young carers who look after parents or older or younger family members.

Hub of Hope – is specific search engine that helps a massive cross section of people with all manner of different problems in their lives. A great deal of what is available here won't be relevant to you – *but equally, a great deal might be.* www.hubofhope.co.uk

Samaritans – www.samaritans.org – when you are in a crisis and you don't know who to turn to, who to speak to or how to find help, call the Samaritans. You can call the Samaritans free from *any* phone on 116 123.

Being Gay is Ok – www.bgiok.org.uk – having a crisis about your sexual orientation and/or identity or gender? You can call for advice on 01483 727667 on Tuesdays and Sundays between 7.30PM and 10PM. Their website has a huge amount of advice available 24/7.

Stonewall – Advice and guidance for the LGBTQIA+ community. Stonewall can help with coming out and with hate crime. 0800 050 2020 www.stonewall.org.uk

Crimestoppers – Would you like to give information anonymously to help solve a crime related problem in your community? Call 0800 555 111. It's always anonymous and safe. www.crimestoppers-uk.org

Fearless – A branch of CrimeStoppers dedicated to young people. www.crimestoppers-uk.org/fearless

Age UK – Worried about an elderly relative that needs support? Contact Age UK www.ageuk.org.uk or call them on 0800 678 1602 between 8AM and 7PM any day of the year.

Carers Trust – If you care for younger siblings or maybe for elderly relatives it might help you to visit Carers Trust – www.carers.org. You can also call them on 0300 772 9600.

Cruse Bereavement Support – If you have lost a loved one and you're struggling to process and deal with that loss, it is understandable. You should seek help and support. Bereavement – the loss of a loved one – is one of the hardest things that life can throw at you. Visit www.cruse.org.uk or call 0808 808 1677. There is help and support available.

Child Bereavement UK – 0800 02 888 40 – www.childbereavementuk.org Child Bereavement UK provide support and assistance on a confidential basis to anyone who needs it. You can also participate in online live chats with specialist advisors.

Pregnancy Crisis Helpline – If you've just found out that you're pregnant the Pregnancy Crisis Helpline can give you support, advice and guidance. You can speak to them confidentially on 0800 368 9296. www.pregnancycrisishelpline.org.uk.

GP Services – When you need a doctor, but you don't know how to find one, visit www.nhs.uk/service-search/find-a-gp. All you have to do is enter your postcode and all of the doctors surgeries in your local area will be identified. There is also advice and guidance on how to register.

The Anti-Bullying Alliance – If you're being bullied in school or in the community – you don't have to tolerate it and we can put an end to it. Bullying ruins lives. Don't let it ruin yours! Visit www.anti-bullyingalliance.org.uk

National Bullying Helpline – 0300 323 0169 / 0845 225 5787 (9AM to 5PM Monday to Friday). Support and assistance for anyone suffering with bullying. It can happen to anyone. Visit www.nationalbullyinghelpline.co.uk

Shelter – If you or a loved one are facing the prospect of becoming homeless, or if you have been sleeping rough or between different addresses – call the Shelter emergency helpline on 0808 800 4444.

YMCA – the YMCA is a charity that specialises in supporting young people from every walk of life and any background. There are YMCA centres in most cities across the UK and you can find a list by visiting www.ymca.org.uk

Barnardo's – www.barnardos.org.uk. A national children's support charity that can help with almost any difficulty that you might have.

About the Author:

Phil Priestley is former police offer who served with North Yorkshire Police and then Cambridgeshire Constabulary for 17 years. Leaving policing in 2019 he setup Inclusive Development Ltd (www.inclusive-development.co.uk), a company that specialises in working with young people in educational settings.

Today Phil works coaching and mentoring young people across the region of Cambridgeshire, Bedfordshire, and North Essex. He has written two books on the threat of County Lines, and is currently studying an MSc in Child and Adolescent Mental Health with the University of Edinburgh. Phil delivers informational presentations across an array of subjects include drugs, criminal exploitation, violence, personal safety, hate crime and more.

Phil is also the founder of a not-for-profit organisation based in Cambridgeshire – the Cambs Youth Panel (www.cambsyouthpanel.co.uk) – which has won several awards for the work it has done helping disadvantaged families through the COVID-19 pandemic, including a regional award from the BBC.

In 2022 Phil was recognised by seven Members of Parliament with a regional award for his contribution to supporting communities throughout the Covid-19 pandemic.

All rights reserved. No part of this publication may be reproduced distributed or transmitted in any form or by any means, including photocopying, recording or other electronic or mechanical methods without the prior written permission of the publisher except in the case of brief quotations embodied in critical reviews and certain other non-commercial uses permitted by copyright law. For permission requests please email the publisher addressed "Attention: Permissions Coordinator" at the following address:

SMP@inclusived-development.co.uk

The characters of 'Katie and Jez' are property of the author and may not be reproduced or used without permission.

Copyright © Philip Priestley 2023.

www.ingramcontent.com/pod-product-compliance
Lightning Source LLC
Chambersburg PA
CBHW042047280426
43661CB00121B/1498/J